OPTIMIZING PROMPT ENGINEERING FOR GENERATIVE AI

OPTIMIZING PROMPT ENGINEERING FOR GENERATIVE AI

Erik Herman

MERCURY LEARNING AND INFORMATION
Boston, Massachusetts

MERCURY LEARNING AND INFORMATION
121 High Street, 3rd Floor
Boston, MA 02110
info@merclearning.com

E. Herman. *Optimizing Prompt Engineering for Generative AI*
ISBN: 978-1-5015-2369-4

Library of Congress Control Number: 2024952457

242526321   This book is printed on acid-free paper in the United States of America.

Our titles are available for adoption, license, or bulk purchase by institutions, corporations, etc. For additional information, please contact the Customer Service At info@merclearning.com

CONTENTS

PREFACE

As artificial intelligence continues to permeate various facets of our lives—from customer service to healthcare and beyond—the ability to effectively communicate with these systems becomes increasingly critical. The art and science of prompt engineering, the practice of designing and refining the inputs that guide AI responses, is at the heart of this interaction. This book, *Optimizing Prompt Engineering for Generative AI*, provides a comprehensive guide to mastering this essential skill. Through theoretical insights and hands-on exercises, it equips readers to unlock the full potential of conversational AI.

Why This Book?

The rapid advancements in AI technology and its widespread adoption across diverse applications have made effective prompt engineering a necessity. Designing prompts that elicit accurate, relevant, and engaging responses is increasingly complex as AI systems become more sophisticated. This book addresses the challenge by offering a detailed exploration of the principles and practices that underpin successful prompt engineering, serving as a practical resource for AI professionals and enthusiasts alike.

What Will You Find Here?

This book combines theoretical concepts with actionable techniques, progressively building your understanding of prompt engineering. Below is a summary of the chapters:

Chapter 1: Introduction to Prompt Engineering introduces the foundational concepts of prompt engineering, emphasizing its role in shaping AI applications. It details the key components of prompts, such as instructions, system messages, and user messages, and explores how their design influences AI behavior. Sample datasets and Python scripts are provided to guide readers in constructing effective prompts.

Chapter 2: Crafting Effective Prompts focuses on creating prompts that are clear, concise, and contextually relevant. It presents strategies for tailoring prompts to specific applications and introduces formats like cloze style, instruction-based, and hybrid prompts. This chapter includes datasets and Python exercises to refine your prompt crafting skills.

Chapter 3: Prompts and Contextual Understanding delves into setting conversational context and tone using system messages. Techniques for enhancing contextual comprehension through prompt augmentation are explained, with exercises for building and analyzing context-driven prompts to improve AI interactions.

Chapter 4: Fine-Tuning Prompts for Specific Use Cases addresses domain-specific challenges in prompt design, integrating specialized knowledge to optimize AI responses. It emphasizes ethical considerations, including strategies for bias mitigation, and guides readers through iterative refinement of prompts using feedback. Domain-specific datasets and Python files are included for practical application.

Chapter 5: Monitoring and Evaluating Prompt Performance explores methods for evaluating conversational AI responses using key metrics and user feedback. Real-world examples of iterative improvement highlight best practices, supported by scripts and datasets to help readers analyze AI-generated outputs.

Chapter 6: Advanced Prompt Engineering Techniques examines sophisticated methods such as temperature adjustments, sampling strategies, and response style customization. The trade-offs between response quality, diversity, and consistency are discussed, with Python exercises for experimenting with advanced techniques.

Chapter 7: Hands-on Exercises and Case Studies provides practical exercises and real-world case studies that showcase the transformative potential of effective prompt engineering. Readers engage with detailed datasets, prompts, and Python scripts for immersive, hands-on exploration.

Chapter 8: Best Practices and Future Directions concludes the book with a review of essential best practices for prompt engineering. It highlights emerging trends in conversational AI, encouraging continuous learning and experimentation through resources like datasets and Python notebooks.

How Is This Book Presented?

Each chapter combines theoretical insights with practical guidance. Fundamental concepts are explained to build a solid foundation, followed by real-world examples and case studies that illustrate these concepts in action. Interactive exercises, leveraging sample datasets and Python scripts, reinforce learning and provide opportunities for experimentation.

Best Practices and Emerging Trends

The book's final chapter presents a roadmap for incorporating best practices into prompt engineering workflows. It also explores advancements in AI and future directions in conversational AI and prompt optimization, ensuring readers remain at the cutting edge of this dynamic field.

Encouraging Continuous Learning and Experimentation

AI evolves rapidly, and staying informed is essential. This book equips readers not only with the tools to excel in prompt engineering but also fosters curiosity and engagement with the broader AI community, encouraging contributions to the field's growth.

A Collaborative Effort

The insights in this book are the product of extensive research and collaboration with AI experts and practitioners. Whether you are a seasoned professional or a beginner, Prompt Engineering for Generative AI: Optimizing Conversational AI is designed to be a practical and valuable companion, guiding you through the complexities of prompt engineering while fostering creativity and ethical responsibility.

Welcome to this journey. Together, let us explore the exciting possibilities and challenges in the world of AI and prompt engineering.

Companion files for this book may be obtained by writing to the publisher at info@merclearning.com.

## CHAPTER 1

INTRODUCTION TO PROMPT ENGINEERING

This chapter introduces the foundational concept of prompt engineering, a critical discipline in the development and enhancement of generative AI systems. As AI continues to permeate various aspects of our lives, the ability to craft effective prompts has become essential in shaping AI behavior and improving outcomes across a wide range of applications.

Prompt engineering is not just a technical skill; it is an art that involves a deep understanding of language, context, and user intent. Well-designed prompts can guide AI systems to produce more accurate, relevant, and user-aligned responses, thereby enhancing the overall performance and reliability of these systems. This chapter provides a comprehensive understanding of prompt engineering, highlighting its pivotal role in driving the effectiveness of generative AI.

Through detailed explanations and practical examples, the exploration will cover how prompts influence AI behavior, the key components of a prompt, and best practices for designing prompts that yield optimal results. By the end of this chapter, readers will have a solid grasp of the principles and techniques of prompt engineering, equipping them with the knowledge to harness the full potential of generative AI in various applications.

DEFINITION AND IMPACT OF PROMPT ENGINEERING ON AI APPLICATIONS

Prompt engineering involves the strategic formulation of inputs that direct AI systems, especially those employing machine learning and generative models, toward generating specific desired outputs. The structure and quality of these prompts are pivotal, affecting the AI's performance and its applicability in diverse fields.

EXTENDED IMPACTS ON AI APPLICATIONS

The extended impacts on AI applications include:

- *Enhancement of Model Accuracy*

  Precisely crafted prompts equip AI models to deliver more accurate responses by incorporating detailed, context-rich cues that diminish ambiguities.

- *Optimization of Training and Execution*

  Efficient prompt design streamlines interactions between users and AI systems, reducing computational demands and hastening response times.

- *Improvement of User Experience*

  By fostering the generation of more targeted and useful responses, prompt engineering bolsters user trust and satisfaction, key metrics for the success of AI implementations.

- *Versatility Across Various Domains*

  Custom prompts allow a single AI model to function effectively across different domains, adapting to the unique requirements of tasks ranging from simple customer inquiries to complex analytical challenges in research.

COMPONENTS OF A PROMPT

A well-constructed prompt in the context of generative AI typically comprises several critical components that collectively guide the AI's response mechanisms, which are:

- *Instructions*

  These articulate the specific tasks that the AI is expected to perform, setting clear expectations for the nature and scope of the AI's response.

- *System Message*

  Includes contextual or background information that equips the AI with necessary details about the environment or scenario pertinent to the task at hand.

- *User Message*

  Represents the direct input from the user, such as queries, commands, or other forms of interaction, which the AI must address or respond to.

A deep understanding of how each component influences the AI's responses is essential for crafting effective prompts that optimize functionality and user engagement.

INFLUENCE OF PROMPT DESIGN ON THE BEHAVIOR OF GENERATIVE AI

The strategic design of prompts is crucial in molding the AI's behavior and output quality. Effective prompt design ensures predictable, reliable, and contextually relevant interactions, whereas inadequate designs may lead to vague or off-target AI responses.

DETAILED EXPLORATION OF KEY INFLUENCES

This section provides detailed information on key influences, including:

- *Precision and Clarity*

  Clear, well-articulated prompts reduce risks of misinterpretation, leading to responses that closely match user intentions.

- *Context Awareness*

  Incorporating comprehensive contextual information within prompts enhances the AI's ability to generate relevant and situational responses, thereby improving the practical utility of AI interactions.

BIAS MITIGATION

Carefully crafted prompts can steer AI responses away from inherent biases, promoting fairness and ethical usage in AI outputs.

The process of designing effective prompts is both an art and a science, requiring a nuanced understanding of AI capabilities and limitations. This craft is becoming increasingly vital as AI technologies advance and integrate more deeply into various aspects of human activity.

CASE STUDIES

The following case studies are designed to provide additional context and detail related to the concepts and topics presented in this chapter. The case studies in this chapter are:

- Case Study 1 – E-commerce Chatbot Enhancement
- Case Study 2 – Healthcare Virtual Assistant

Case Study 1 – E-commerce Chatbot Enhancement

Objective

Refine an e-commerce chatbot's prompts to enhance customer engagement and satisfaction.

Challenge

The e-commerce chatbot initially struggled to meet customer expectations due to its vague and unhelpful responses. This lack of precision in its communication led to user frustration and low satisfaction ratings. Customers often found the chatbot's responses to be ambiguous, which hindered their ability to find the products or information they were seeking. The primary challenge was to redesign the chatbot's prompts to be more intuitive, context-aware, and user-friendly.

Solution

To address these issues, the chatbot's prompts underwent a comprehensive revision process. The key steps in this solution included:

- *Assessment of Existing Prompts*

  Analyzing the current prompts to identify specific areas where the responses were falling short. This involved reviewing customer feedback, interaction logs, and common points of confusion.

- *Incorporation of Clearer Instructions*

  Redesigning the prompts to provide more explicit and straightforward instructions. This meant using language that was easy to understand and directly addressed common customer queries.

- *Context-Specific Cues*

  Integrating context-specific information to make the responses more relevant to the user's situation. For example, if a customer were looking for a specific product, the chatbot would now ask clarifying questions about preferences, budget, and previous purchases to tailor its recommendations more accurately.

- *Iterative Testing and Refinement*

  Implementing the new prompts in a controlled environment and collecting data on their effectiveness. This phase involved continuous monitoring and iterative adjustments based on real-world user interactions and feedback.

Outcome

The refined prompts significantly improved the chatbot's performance. Key outcomes included:

- *Increased Clarity and Relevance*

  The revised prompts provided clearer and more relevant information, which directly addressed the customers' needs. This reduced confusion and made the chatbot interactions more productive.

- *Enhanced User Experience*

  Customers experienced a more seamless and intuitive interaction with the chatbot. The context-specific cues helped the chatbot understand and respond more accurately to user inquiries, enhancing overall user satisfaction.

- *Quantifiable Improvements*

  The changes led to a 30% increase in successful interactions, as measured by the completion of customer queries and positive feedback. Additionally, customer satisfaction ratings saw a marked improvement, reflecting the enhanced quality of the chatbot's assistance.

- *Business Impact*

  The improvement in customer engagement and satisfaction translated into better customer retention and potentially higher sales, as satisfied customers were more likely to complete their purchases and return for future transactions.

This case study underscores the importance of prompt engineering in enhancing the effectiveness of AI-driven customer service tools. By focusing on clarity, context, and continuous improvement, businesses can significantly boost the performance of their AI systems and deliver superior customer experiences.

Case Study 2 – Healthcare Virtual Assistant

Objective

Implement a healthcare virtual assistant designed to guide patients through the pre-appointment processes efficiently and clearly.

Challenge

Patients frequently encountered confusion due to complex medical terminology and detailed process descriptions provided by the virtual assistant. This confusion led to difficulties in completing pre-appointment requirements, resulting in missed steps, incorrect information submissions, and overall frustration. The primary challenge was to simplify the virtual assistant's prompts to make them easily understandable for patients without medical knowledge, thereby ensuring a smooth and stress-free pre-appointment experience.

Solution

The solution involved a multifaceted approach to overhaul the virtual assistant's prompts, focusing on clarity, simplicity, and user-friendliness. Key steps included:

* *Assessment of Current Prompts*

    A thorough review of the existing prompts was conducted to pinpoint areas where medical jargon and complex instructions were causing confusion. Feedback from patients and healthcare staff was instrumental in identifying the most problematic areas.

* *Simplification of Language*

    The prompts were rewritten using plain language, avoiding medical jargon and technical terms. The goal was to ensure that any patient, regardless of their background or familiarity with medical processes, could easily understand the instructions.

* *Use of Visual Aids*

    Where possible, visual aids such as icons, diagrams, and step-by-step guides were incorporated to complement the text prompts. These visual elements helped illustrate procedures and instructions, making them more intuitive.

* *Contextual Prompts*

    Prompts were tailored to be context-specific, providing relevant information based on the patient's current step in the pre-appointment process. This approach minimized information overload and allowed patients to focus on one task at a time.

- *Iterative Testing and Feedback*

  The revised prompts were tested with a diverse group of patients to gather feedback on their clarity and effectiveness. Continuous adjustments were made based on this feedback to refine the prompts further.

Outcome

The implementation of simplified and clarified prompts led to several significant improvements:

- *Enhanced Patient Compliance*

  Patients found the new prompts much easier to follow, which resulted in higher compliance rates with pre-appointment requirements. They were able to complete necessary steps accurately and efficiently.

- *Reduced Confusion and Frustration*

  The use of plain language and visual aids reduced the confusion and frustration previously experienced by patients. The clear and straightforward instructions made the process less daunting and more manageable.

- *Operational Efficiency*

  With patients better prepared and informed before their appointments, there was a noticeable reduction in the administrative workload for healthcare staff. Staff spent less time clarifying instructions and correcting mistakes, allowing them to focus on more critical tasks.

- *Improved Patient Satisfaction*

  The overall patient experience improved, as evidenced by positive feedback and higher satisfaction ratings. Patients appreciated the user-friendly interface and clear guidance provided by the virtual assistant.

- *Positive Impact on Healthcare Delivery*

  By ensuring patients arrived at their appointments well-prepared and with the necessary information, the healthcare facility could deliver more efficient and effective care. This improvement contributed to better patient outcomes and a smoother operational flow.

This case study highlights the critical role of prompt engineering in enhancing the functionality and user experience of AI-driven healthcare tools. By prioritizing simplicity and clarity in prompt design, healthcare providers can significantly improve patient interactions with virtual assistants, leading to better compliance, satisfaction, and overall efficiency.

TUTORIALS AND HANDS-ON EXERCISES

The following tutorials and hands-on exercises are designed to provide practical experience and application of the concepts and topics presented in this chapter. The tutorials and hands-on exercises in this chapter are:

- Exercise 1 – Crafting Your First Prompt
- Exercise 2 – Evaluating Prompt Effectiveness

Exercise 1 – Crafting Your First Prompt

Objective

In this exercise, you will create a prompt for a movie recommendation system. Follow the steps to craft an effective prompt that helps the AI understand the user's preferences and provide relevant recommendations.

Steps

Step 1 – Define the User's Intent

Start by identifying what the user wants from the movie recommendation system. For example, the user might want to find a new movie to watch based on their favorite genre or recent viewing history.

Example

The user's intent is to find a comedy movie like ones they have enjoyed in the past.

Step 2 – Create Clear Instructions for the AI

Provide specific and clear instructions to guide the AI in understanding and fulfilling the user's request. Make sure the instructions are easy to understand and leave no room for ambiguity.

Example

"Please recommend a comedy movie that is similar to 'The Hangover' and 'Superbad'."

Step 3 – Include Contextual Information to Help the AI Understand the User's Preferences

Adding contextual information about the user's preferences or past interactions can help the AI make more accurate recommendations.

Example

"I enjoy light-hearted and humorous movies with a lot of funny dialogues. I have recently watched and liked 'The Hangover' and 'Superbad'.

Putting It All Together

Combining the previous steps, the complete prompt for the movie recommendation system might look like this:

"Please recommend a comedy movie that is like 'The Hangover' and 'Superbad'. I enjoy light-hearted and humorous movies with a lot of funny dialogues. I have recently watched and liked 'The Hangover' and 'Superbad'."

Additional Tips

- Be specific about the genres or themes you like.
- Mention any recent movies you have enjoyed, giving the AI more context.
- Keep the instructions clear and concise to avoid confusion.

By following these steps, you will be able to create a prompt that effectively communicates your intent and preferences to the AI, leading to better and more relevant movie recommendations.

Exercise 2 – Evaluating Prompt Effectiveness

Objective

In this exercise, you will learn how to evaluate and improve the effectiveness of a prompt by identifying its weaknesses, redesigning it, and comparing AI responses before and after the modification.

Steps

Step 1 – Identify Weaknesses in the Original Prompt

Start by analyzing the original prompt to identify any areas that may be unclear, ambiguous, or lacking in detail. Look for parts that could lead to misunderstanding or irrelevant responses from the AI.

Original Prompt Example
"Recommend a movie."

Weaknesses

- Too vague and lacks specificity.
- Does not provide any context or user preferences.
- May result in random or irrelevant movie suggestions.

Step 2 – Redesign the Prompt to Address These Weaknesses

Modify the original prompt to make it more specific, clear, and context rich. Ensure the prompt provides enough information for the AI to understand the user's intent and preferences.

Redesigned Prompt Example

"Please recommend a science fiction movie that has a strong female lead and a captivating storyline. I recently enjoyed 'Arrival' and 'Gravity'."

Improvements

- Specifies the genre (science fiction).
- Includes user preferences (strong female lead, captivating storyline).
- Provides examples of movies the user liked (Arrival, Gravity).

Step 3 – Compare AI Responses Before and After the Modification

Evaluate the AI's responses to both the original and redesigned prompts. Compare the relevance and quality of the recommendations to determine the effectiveness of the modifications.

AI Response to Original Prompt
Random movie recommendation, e.g., "I recommend 'Inception'."

AI Response to Redesigned Prompt

▪ Relevant movie recommendation, e.g., "I recommend 'The Martian', which features a strong female lead and a gripping plot, like 'Arrival' and 'Gravity'."

Comparison

▪ The original prompt resulted in a random suggestion without considering the user's preferences.

▪ The redesigned prompt provided a relevant and targeted recommendation based on the user's specified criteria and past preferences.

By following these steps, you can effectively evaluate and enhance the clarity and effectiveness of prompts, leading to more accurate and satisfying responses from the AI.

PROMPTS IN PRACTICE: A SIMPLE AI PROMPT

This section provides examples and information for implementing the prompt engineering concepts and topics presented in this chapter, including a Python script, sample data, and steps for testing and validating the code.

Python Script

Basic script (see Figure 1.1) demonstrating how to implement and test a simple AI prompt.

```python
# Basic AI Prompt Implementation Script

import openai

# Set up your OpenAI API key
openai.api_key = 'INSERT API KEY'

def send_prompt(prompt):
    response = openai.Completion.create(
        engine="davinci",
        prompt=prompt,
        max_tokens=150
    )
    return response.choices[0].text.strip()

def main():
    # Example prompt
    prompt = "What are the benefits of regular exercise?"
    response = send_prompt(prompt)
    print("AI Response:", response)

if __name__ == "__main__":
    main()
```

FIGURE 1.1 Basic AI prompt implementation script.

Code Explanation: Basic AI Prompt Implementation Script

This script demonstrates how to use Python to interact with the OpenAI API, allowing users to send prompts and receive AI-generated responses. Here's a detailed explanation tailored for learners interested in prompt engineering:

1. Importing the OpenAI Library

   The script begins by importing the *"openai"* library. This library provides the necessary functions to interact with OpenAI's language models. Importing this library is essential to use its features.

2. Setting Up the API Key

   An API key is required to authenticate your requests to the OpenAI service. In this script, the *"openai.api_key"* variable is set with your unique API key. This key is a string of characters provided by OpenAI and must be kept secure. Replacing the placeholder with your actual API key enables you to access OpenAI's models.

3. Defining the "send_prompt" Function

   The *"send_prompt"* function is defined to handle sending prompts to the OpenAI API and processing the responses. The function accepts a single parameter, *"prompt"*, which is the text you want the AI to respond to.
   Inside the function, the *"openai.Completion.create"* method is called. This method sends a request to OpenAI's language model specified by the *"model"* parameter (in this case, *"text-davinci-003"*). The *"prompt"* parameter contains the text you want the AI to respond to, and *"max_tokens"* limits the length of the AI's response to 150 tokens.
   The function processes the API's response by accessing the *"choices"* array and retrieving the text of the first choice. This text is then stripped of any leading or trailing whitespace using the *"strip()"* method before being returned.

4. Main Function

   The *"main"* function is defined to demonstrate an example usage of the *"send_prompt"* function. Within this function, an example prompt asking about the benefits of regular exercise is defined. The *"send_prompt"* function is called with this prompt, and the resulting response from the AI is printed to the console.

5. Script Execution

   The final part of the script ensures that the *"main"* function is called when the script is run directly. This is achieved using the *"if __name__ == "__main__":"* construct. It checks if the script is being executed as the main module and, if so, calls the "main" function.

Key Concepts for Prompt Engineering Learners

▪ *API Setup*: Understanding how to configure and use an API key to authenticate requests.

▪ *Function Creation*: Learning how to create and utilize functions to modularize code, making it reusable and easier to manage.

▪ *Prompt Crafting*: Seeing the impact of different prompt structures and how they influence the AI's responses. Crafting clear and concise prompts is crucial for effective prompt engineering.

▪ *Response Handling*: Learning how to process and clean up the AI's response to make it presentable and useful.

Datasets

Sample Data

A dataset of user interactions with a virtual travel booking assistant, useful for testing prompt refinements.

Example from dataset:

```
[
    {
        "interaction_id": 1,
        "user_input": "I want to book a flight from New York to Los Angeles next week.",
        "assistant_response": "Sure! Can you please provide the exact date of your departure?"
    },
```

CONCLUSION

As artificial intelligence continues its rapid evolution, the importance of prompt engineering is becoming increasingly evident. This discipline is emerging as a pivotal factor in enhancing the effectiveness and reliability of AI applications across diverse industries. The thoughtful design and crafting of prompts are not merely about improving immediate outputs; they are about guiding the AI's developmental trajectory, ensuring more accurate, relevant, and user-aligned responses.

In the realm of AI, prompt engineering is akin to the art of asking the right questions. It involves understanding the nuances of language, the context of queries, and the underlying intent of users. This skill set is essential for bridging the gap between human expectations and machine capabilities. Effective prompts can significantly enhance user satisfaction, leading to better engagement and trust in AI systems.

The implications of mastering prompt engineering are profound. For instance, in healthcare, precisely designed prompts can enable AI systems to provide more accurate diagnoses and personalized treatment recommendations. In finance, they can help in generating more reliable risk assessments and investment strategies. In customer service, well-crafted prompts can lead to faster and more satisfactory resolutions of customer issues.

Moreover, prompt engineering is not just about current applications; it is also about shaping the future of AI. As we move toward more advanced AI models, such as those incorporating natural language understanding and generation at deeper levels, the role of prompt engineering will become even more critical. It will be essential for refining AI models, reducing biases, and enhancing their interpretability and fairness.

For AI practitioners and developers, acquiring skills in prompt engineering is not optional but necessary. It is a strategic investment in their professional toolkit, enabling them to harness the full potential of AI technologies. As the field of AI continues to expand, those proficient in prompt engineering will be at the forefront, driving innovations and setting new standards for AI-human interactions.

Looking ahead, the trajectory of AI development suggests that prompt engineering will play a significant role in upcoming advancements. With continuous improvements in AI algorithms and the growing complexity of AI applications, the demand for sophisticated prompt engineering techniques will only increase. This evolution will lead to AI systems that are more intuitive, responsive, and aligned with human needs, paving the way for groundbreaking applications that we can only begin to imagine today.

In conclusion, as AI becomes more integrated into our daily lives, the significance of prompt engineering cannot be overstated. It is the key to unlocking the next level of AI capabilities, ensuring that these technologies are not only powerful but also accessible, ethical, and aligned with human values. By mastering prompt engineering, we are not just improving AI systems; we are shaping the future of human–AI collaboration.

## CHAPTER 2

CRAFTING EFFECTIVE PROMPTS

The effectiveness of AI systems hinges significantly on the quality and design of the prompts they process. This chapter investigates the methodologies for developing effective prompts that align with the contextual requirements and desired outcomes of AI applications. Crafting well-designed prompts is crucial for enhancing the interaction between AI and users, influencing AI behavior, and optimizing response quality.

The performance of AI systems is deeply influenced by how well prompts are tailored to the specific situational context and the operational behavior of the AI. An effective prompt considers the comprehensive environment in which the AI operates, including user intent, relevant historical data, and the specific tasks being addressed. This contextual sensitivity ensures that AI responses are not only accurate but also highly relevant to the user's needs.

Predictability in AI responses is vital, particularly in environments where consistency and reliability are critical, such as regulatory compliance and safety-critical operations. Understanding the AI's underlying algorithms and operational logic allows for the creation of prompts that yield predictable and stable outcomes. This predictability enhances compliance with standards and builds user trust in the AI system.

One of the key aspects of crafting effective prompts is the ability to customize them based on individual user needs and histories. By integrating data from previous interactions, AI systems can provide highly personalized responses that anticipate user preferences and requirements. This level of customization is essential in fields like e-commerce and personalized healthcare, where user satisfaction and engagement are directly influenced by the AI's ability to cater to unique user profiles.

Clear and unambiguous instructions are the foundation of effective AI prompts. The balance between brevity and completeness is crucial to prevent overwhelming both the AI and the user. Using direct, action-oriented language and avoiding ambiguity ensures that AI systems deliver precise and useful responses. Incorporating feedback loops further enhances clarity and performance, allowing AI to request additional information when needed to complete tasks effectively.

Different prompt formats serve distinct purposes and can dramatically influence the outcome of an AI's task execution. This chapter introduces various prompt formats, including cloze style, instruction-based, and hybrid prompts. Each format is tailored to leverage AI capabilities for specific operational needs, and understanding their strategic application is key to optimizing AI–user interactions.

The chapter includes case studies that illustrate the practical application and impact of well-designed prompts in different AI scenarios. These examples highlight how strategic prompt design can enhance AI functionality, improve user satisfaction, and drive more meaningful interactions. By focusing on personalization, specificity, and contextual awareness, these case studies demonstrate the transformative potential of optimized prompts.

To deepen your understanding of prompt engineering, the chapter provides practical exercises that focus on improving contextual sensitivity and clarity. These exercises are designed to help you develop skills in crafting and refining AI prompts, ensuring that AI systems can deliver more accurate and user-tailored responses. Additionally, online supplemental materials, including code examples, datasets, and further reading links, support the practical application of the concepts covered in this chapter.

By mastering the methodologies and techniques outlined in this chapter, developers and AI practitioners can enhance the effectiveness and efficiency of their AI systems. This strategic approach to prompt engineering not only optimizes the functionality of AI applications but also fosters a more intuitive and responsive interaction landscape, leading to better user experiences and outcomes.

6

THE ROLE OF CONTEXT AND SYSTEM BEHAVIOR IN CRAFTING EFFECTIVE PROMPTS

The efficacy of AI interactions is heavily reliant on the quality of the prompts it processes. These prompts, when meticulously tailored to match the specific situational context and the operational behavior of the AI system, significantly elevate the system's performance, including:

▪ Contextual Sensitivity

The design of an effective prompt requires an acute awareness of the comprehensive environment in which the AI operates. This includes a thorough consideration of environmental factors, the user's intent, relevant historical data, and the specific tasks being addressed. Such a holistic view ensures that the AI can finely tune its responses to align perfectly with the intricacies of the situation, which enhances both the relevance and the accuracy of its outputs. For example, a prompt for a customer service AI might integrate recent purchase history and any ongoing issues to tailor the conversation, thereby making the interaction more relevant and efficient.

Example Prompt

"Given the customer's recent purchase of a laptop and reported issues with battery life, provide troubleshooting advice and warranty options."

▪ Predictability in Responses

The ability to predict how an AI will respond under various circumstances is pivotal, especially in environments where consistency and reliability are paramount, such as regulatory compliance or safety-critical operations. By understanding the underlying algorithms and operational logic of the AI, developers can craft prompts that exploit these mechanisms to yield predictable and stable outcomes. This predictability not only ensures compliance with standards but also builds user trust in AI applications.

Example Prompt

"Generate a monthly compliance report detailing all deviations from the standard operating procedures in the manufacturing line as per the latest safety regulations."

▪ Customization for User Needs

Tailoring prompts to the specific needs and histories of individual users can drastically enhance the personalized nature of AI responses. By integrating data from previous interactions, the AI can provide responses that are not only relevant but also anticipate the user's needs and preferences. This level of personalization is crucial in domains such as e-commerce or personalized healthcare, where user satisfaction and engagement are directly correlated with the system's ability to cater to unique user profiles.

Example Prompt

"Review the user's previous health inquiries and current medication list to provide personalized health advice for managing seasonal allergies."

These aspects of prompt crafting underscore the necessity for a deep understanding of both the technical and situational layers that influence AI behavior. By mastering these elements, developers and AI practitioners can ensure their systems operate not only with high efficiency but also with an attuned sense of context and user-centricity. This strategic approach to prompt engineering not only optimizes the functionality of AI systems but also enhances the overall user experience, fostering a more intuitive and responsive interaction landscape.

IMPORTANCE AND CHARACTERISTICS OF CLEAR USER INSTRUCTIONS

Clear and unambiguous instructions are the cornerstone of effective AI prompts. They play a pivotal role in minimizing user confusion and ensuring that AI systems deliver precise and useful responses. Mastering the art of crafting such instructions is essential for optimizing the interaction between humans and machines, including:

- Conciseness and Clarity

   The most effective prompts strike a delicate balance between brevity and completeness. Instructions should be concise enough to be easily digestible and clear enough to convey all necessary information. This balance is crucial to prevent overwhelming both the AI and the user, which can detract from the AI's ability to process and respond accurately. For example, instructions for an AI assistant in customer service should be straightforward, directing the AI to not only respond to queries but also to provide additional relevant information, such as related products or services.

Example Prompt

"Inform the customer about the features of the product they are inquiring about and suggest similar products in our range."

■ Action-Oriented Language

Utilizing direct and action-oriented language in prompts helps in guiding the AI with precision. This approach fosters clear directives and ensures goal-directed responses that are aligned with the user's objectives. It is particularly effective in operational environments where specific actions are required from the AI, like issuing commands in industrial automation or executing financial transactions.

Example Prompt

"Calculate the total cost for the customer's shopping cart and apply any available loyalty discounts."

■ Avoidance of Ambiguity

The clarity of instructions also plays a critical role in eliminating ambiguity, ensuring that the AI's responses are both accurate and relevant. This is especially important in high-stakes fields such as medical diagnostics or legal advice, where the precision of the information provided can have significant consequences. Clear instructions help in mitigating risks associated with misinterpretations, thus enhancing the reliability and trustworthiness of the AI system.

Example Prompt

"Provide a step-by-step guide for administering the prescribed medication, including dosage and frequency."

■ Incorporating Feedback Loops

To further enhance the clarity of instructions, incorporating feedback mechanisms can be highly beneficial. These loops allow the AI to request clarification if an instruction is unclear or if additional information is needed to complete a task effectively. This not only improves the quality of the AI's performance but also adapts the system to better meet user needs over time.

Example Prompt

"If the patient's symptoms are unclear, ask for specific details about the duration and intensity of the symptoms."

By integrating these characteristics into prompt design, developers can improve the functionality and user experience of AI systems. Clear, concise, and action-oriented instructions are fundamental in creating interactions that are efficient, effective, and user-friendly.

INTRODUCTION TO VARIOUS PROMPT FORMATS

Selecting the most effective prompt format is crucial for optimizing interactions between AI systems and users. Different formats serve distinct purposes and can dramatically influence the outcome of an AI's task execution and decision-making processes. Here, we explore the most used prompt formats, each tailored to leverage AI capabilities for specific operational needs.

Cloze Style Prompts

Cloze style prompts are especially useful for information retrieval or data completion tasks. They are designed with blank spaces that the AI needs to fill in, based on the surrounding context. This format is particularly effective in testing and enhancing an AI's comprehension and predictive abilities.

Example Prompt

"The current President of the United States is ____ and he succeeded ____."

Advantages

By necessitating that the AI deduces the missing information from given cues, cloze prompts are excellent for reinforcing learning models that depend on context clues.

Instruction-Based Prompts

These prompts are ideal for directive tasks where specific actions are required from the AI. They are clear and direct, asking the AI to execute a particular function, ranging from generating detailed reports to solving complex calculations.

Example Prompt

"Generate a summary of the latest financial news articles focusing on the stock market trends of this week."

Advantages

Instruction-based prompts help in maintaining clarity and focus, directing the AI to deliver precise outputs based on explicit commands. They are particularly useful in structured environments where the desired outcome is well-defined.

Hybrid Prompts

Hybrid prompts integrate elements from both cloze style and instruction-based formats, providing a balanced approach for more complex interaction scenarios. This type is suitable for environments requiring a combination of directive language and contextual understanding, such as in interactive customer service or when dealing with multidomain tasks.

Example Prompt

"Given the user's interest in historical fiction and preference for eBooks, recommend five books that _____ and are rated at least four stars on Goodreads."

Advantages

These prompts offer flexibility and adaptability, making them effective in dynamic situations where the AI must navigate between different types of input and outputs, ensuring both relevance and depth in its responses.

Strategic Application of Different Formats

Each prompt format can be strategically employed based on the specific interaction goals and the nuances of the AI system's training. For instance, cloze style prompts can be used in educational settings to assist in language learning applications, while instruction-based prompts might be more applicable in business analytics tools to process data and provide insights. Hybrid prompts can be particularly useful in customer support bots where both reactive and proactive responses are necessary.

Enhancing AI Training with Diverse Prompt Formats

Utilizing a variety of prompt formats not only improves the immediate functionality of AI systems but also aids in their learning and adaptation processes. By exposing AI to different types of prompts, developers can simulate a range of scenarios that enhance the AI's ability to generalize from its training and apply its learning in real-world applications. This diversification in training prompts ensures that the AI can handle a broader spectrum of tasks and improves its overall robustness and reliability.

Understanding and implementing various prompt formats is key to crafting successful AI–user interactions. Each format brings unique benefits and is suitable for specific types of tasks, playing a critical role in the effectiveness and efficiency of AI systems.

CASE STUDIES

These case studies illustrate the practical application and impact of well-designed prompts in different AI scenarios. They provide insights into how targeted changes to the prompt structure can significantly enhance AI functionality and user experience. The case studies in this chapter are:

- Case Study 1 – Financial Services Bot Improvement
- Case Study 2 – University Admission Query Assistant

Case Study 1 – Financial Services Bot Improvement

Objective

Optimize a financial services bot to enhance client interactions and provide more personalized and actionable financial advice.

Challenge

Clients frequently reported that the bot's advice was too generic and often irrelevant to their specific financial situations. This lack of tailored guidance led to dissatisfaction, reduced engagement, and a decline in trust toward the bot's capabilities. Clients needed more relevant advice that considered their individual financial profiles, recent transactions, and specific inquiries.

Solution

To address these issues, the bot was reprogrammed with more detailed and personalized prompts that aligned closely with the users' financial profiles. Key enhancements included:

- *Integration of User Financial Profiles*

  The bot was updated to consider detailed aspects of the user's financial profile, including their recent transactions, investment history, financial goals, and risk preferences.

- *Detailed and Specific Prompts*

  Prompts were redesigned to be more specific and context aware. For example, instead of asking broadly about investment advice, the bot now includes detailed references to the user's recent financial activities and preferences.

- *Enhanced Data Utilization*

  The bot was equipped with the ability to analyze recent transactions and financial behavior to tailor its advice more accurately. This included recommending investment opportunities that matched the user's risk profile and financial goals.

- *Iterative Testing and Feedback*

  The new prompts were tested in real-world scenarios to gather user feedback. This iterative process ensured that the prompts were continuously refined based on client interactions and satisfaction levels.

Outcome

The implementation of more nuanced and personalized prompts led to several significant improvements:

- *Increased Relevance of Advice*

  The advice provided by the bot became significantly more relevant and actionable, as it was closely aligned with the clients' specific financial situations and goals.

- *Enhanced Client Satisfaction*

  Clients reported higher satisfaction with the bot's advice, noting that it felt more personalized and useful. This improvement was reflected in positive feedback and higher engagement rates.

- *Boost in Trust and Reliance*

  The personalized nature of the prompts helped rebuild trust in the bot's capabilities. Clients began to rely more on the bot for financial guidance, recognizing its ability to provide tailored and valuable advice.

- *Actionable Recommendations*

  The bot's recommendations were not only relevant but also actionable, empowering clients to make informed financial decisions based on their specific circumstances and preferences.

Example Prompt Comparison

- Before

  "What investment advice do you need?"

- After

  "Based on your recent investment in technology stocks and your medium-risk profile, would you like to explore similar opportunities or diversify?"

The before prompt was too broad and lacked the specificity needed to provide useful advice. The after prompt, however, directly referenced the client's recent investment activity and risk profile, offering a choice that felt tailored and relevant.

This case study underscores the transformative impact of prompt engineering on AI-driven financial services. By focusing on personalization and specificity, financial services bots can significantly enhance client interactions, leading to better satisfaction, engagement, and trust. This approach not only improves the user experience but also drives more meaningful and effective financial guidance.

Case Study 2 – University Admission Query Assistant

Objective
Develop an AI-driven query assistant designed to effectively manage and respond to complex inquiries from prospective students.

Challenge
The initial version of the AI assistant faced significant challenges in handling multipart questions and providing comprehensive responses. This inadequacy led to prospective students feeling frustrated and poorly informed, which could potentially deter them from applying. The assistant's inability to deliver detailed answers to complex queries about admission procedures, program specifics, and eligibility criteria was a major obstacle.

Solution
To overcome these issues, the prompts were redesigned into a hybrid format that combined direct instructions with contextual elements. This new approach aimed to guide the AI assistant not only to address the immediate queries but also to incorporate relevant additional information. Key steps in the solution included:

- *Hybrid Prompt Format*

  Redesigning the prompts to include both direct instructions and contextual cues. This ensured that the AI could provide comprehensive responses by pulling in relevant details such as admission deadlines, program specifics, and eligibility criteria.

- *Contextual Awareness*

  Enhancing the AI's ability to understand and respond to multipart questions by breaking down complex queries into manageable parts.

The assistant was programmed to recognize and address multiple facets of a single inquiry, providing a holistic response.

- *Iterative Refinement*

  Continuously testing and refining the prompts based on real-world interactions and feedback from prospective students. This iterative process helped in fine-tuning the AI's responses to be more precise and informative.

- *Enhanced Data Utilization*

  Integrating data about various programs, deadlines, and admission criteria into the AI's knowledge base. This allowed the assistant to access and provide specific information as needed, improving the relevance of its responses.

Outcome

The implementation of these redesigned prompts led to several significant improvements:

- *Improved Response Quality*

  The revised assistant provided much more detailed and relevant answers, significantly enhancing the satisfaction levels among prospective students. The comprehensive responses addressed the students' queries more effectively, leaving them better informed.

- *Increased Efficiency*

  By delivering more accurate and informative answers, the assistant reduced the need for follow-up questions, thereby decreasing the workload on human staff. This allowed the admissions team to focus on more complex inquiries and tasks.

- *Higher Engagement*

  Prospective students engaged more with the AI assistant due to its improved ability to handle complex and multipart questions. This increased engagement is crucial for maintaining interest and encouraging applications.

- *Enhanced User Experience*

  The detailed and contextually aware responses contributed to a more positive user experience. Prospective students felt their concerns were adequately addressed, which fostered a sense of confidence and trust in the institution.

Example Prompt Comparison

- Before

  "What questions do you have about our university?"

- After

  "You asked about the master's in computer science. Would you like to know about the admission requirements or the course details?"

The before prompt was too vague and open-ended, often leading to incomplete or unsatisfactory responses. The after prompt, however, was specific and contextually aware, directly addressing the student's query and providing a clear direction for further information.

Impact and Insights

These case studies demonstrate the transformative potential of optimized prompts in AI systems across different domains. By refining the prompt design to be more specific and contextually aware, AI applications can achieve higher levels of precision and relevance in their interactions. This not only enhances the user experience but also bolsters the overall effectiveness of the AI system, leading to better outcomes in user engagement and operational efficiency. The improvements seen in the university admission query assistant highlight the critical role that well-designed prompts play in ensuring AI systems meet user needs effectively and efficiently.

TUTORIALS AND HANDS-ON EXERCISES

These exercises are designed to deepen your understanding of prompt engineering by providing practical experience in crafting and refining AI prompts. They focus on improving contextual sensitivity and clarity to ensure AI systems can deliver more accurate and user-tailored responses. The tutorials and hands-on exercises in this chapter are:

- Exercise 1 – Create a Set of Prompts for a Weather Information Bot Tailored to User Location and Query Specificity

- Exercise 2 – Revise Prompts for an Existing Customer Support AI to Reduce Ambiguity and Enhance Resolution Effectiveness

Exercise 1 – Create a Set of Prompts for a Weather Information Bot Tailored to User Location and Query Specificity

Objective

In this exercise, you will develop a set of prompts for a weather information bot that tailors its responses based on the user's location and the specificity of their query. Follow the steps below to create effective, context-sensitive prompts.

Steps

Step 1 – Identify Key Information

Determine the critical contextual information that will enhance the bot's responses. This may include:

- *User's Current Location*: Knowing where the user is located or where they are interested in receiving weather information.

- *Type of Weather Information Sought*: Identifying whether the user is asking about temperature, precipitation, humidity, wind conditions, etc.

- *Additional Preferences*: Understanding any specific user preferences, such as alerts for allergies, suitability for outdoor activities, or specific times of day.

Example

A user wants to know the weather forecast for Seattle, including details that will help them plan a hiking trip.

Step 2 – Create Contextual Prompts

Develop prompts that integrate the identified contextual elements. These prompts should guide the AI to provide detailed and relevant information tailored to the user's needs.

Examples

- "Given the user's location in Seattle and their interest in hiking, provide a weather forecast that includes temperature, chance of rain, and pollen count for the next three days."

- "For a user planning to jog in Central Park tomorrow morning, provide a detailed weather forecast including humidity levels and sunrise time."

- "What will the temperature and UV index be at noon in Miami Beach for someone planning to spend the day at the beach?"

Step 3 – Test and Refine

Simulate different user scenarios to test the bot's responses. Use feedback from these simulations to adjust the prompts, ensuring the responses are relevant and specific to the context provided. The goal is to fine-tune the prompts to better meet user needs and enhance the overall user experience.

Testing Process

- *Scenario 1*: A user in New York asks for the weather conditions for a weekend picnic, including temperature, wind speed, and precipitation chance.

- *Scenario 2*: A user in Denver wants to know if it is safe to go for a run tomorrow morning, including temperature, air quality index, and wind conditions.

- *Scenario 3*: A user in Los Angeles requests a weather update for their evening beach outing, focusing on temperature, sunset time, and UV index.

Refinement Based on Feedback

- If users report that the information is too generic, add more specific details such as exact times and additional weather parameters.

- If users find the responses confusing, simplify the language and structure of the prompts to make the information more accessible.

Example Prompt

"For a user planning to jog in Central Park tomorrow morning, provide a detailed weather forecast including humidity levels and sunrise time."

By following these steps, the weather information bot can provide more tailored and contextually relevant responses, enhancing the user experience. This approach ensures that users receive specific, actionable weather information that meets their needs and preferences, leading to higher satisfaction and engagement with the bot.

Exercise 2 – Revise Prompts for an Existing Customer Support AI to Reduce Ambiguity and Enhance Resolution Effectiveness

Exercise

In this exercise, you will revise prompts for a customer support AI to make them clearer and more precise, thereby improving the effectiveness of issue resolution. Use the following steps to refine the prompts and enhance the AI's performance.

Steps

Step 1 – Analyze Current Prompts

Review the existing prompts to identify areas where users frequently encounter confusion or where the AI fails to deliver precise information. Look for patterns in user queries and responses that indicate misunderstandings or inefficiencies.

Example Analysis

Current Prompt: "What can I help you with today?"

Issue Identified: Users often provide vague descriptions of their problems, leading to back-and-forth interactions that delay resolution.

Step 2 – Rewrite Prompts

Update the prompts to be more specific and instructive. Ensure that each prompt clearly communicates the expected action or response from the AI. The goal is to reduce ambiguity and guide users to provide the necessary information upfront.

Examples

- *Current Prompt*: "Handle the customer's query."
- *Rewritten Prompt*: "Provide a step-by-step solution to the customer's issue with their device setup."

- *Current Prompt*: "What can I help you with today?"
- *Rewritten Prompt*: "Please describe the issue with your product, including the model number and the error message received, so I can assist you better."

Step 3 – Evaluate Through Role-Playing

Use role-playing sessions or simulated interactions to test how the new prompts perform. Assess the clarity and effectiveness of the AI's responses under different scenarios and continue refining the prompts based on this feedback.

Testing Process

- *Scenario 1*: A user reports a problem with their internet connection.
- *Scenario 2*: A user needs assistance with setting up a new device.
- *Scenario 3*: A user encounters an error message while using a software application.

Step 4 – Refinement Based on Feedback
If users still experience confusion, further clarify the prompts by providing examples or additional guidance.

If the AI's responses are not sufficiently detailed, include more specific instructions in the prompts to ensure comprehensive assistance.

Example Prompt Comparison

Before
"What can I help you with today?"

After
"Please describe the issue with your product, including the model number and the error message received, so I can assist you better."

Developing Skills Through Practice

Both exercises aim to enhance your ability to design and refine AI prompts that are not only contextually aware but also precise and clear. Through practice, you can develop a keen understanding of how different types of information and phrasing affect the AI's performance. These skills are crucial for anyone looking to improve the interactivity and user satisfaction of AI systems in real-world applications.

By focusing on clarity and precision, you can significantly enhance the effectiveness of customer support AI, leading to faster resolution times, increased user satisfaction, and reduced workload for human support staff. This exercise demonstrates the importance of meticulous prompt design in creating efficient and user-friendly AI interactions.

PROMPTS IN PRACTICE: CONSTRUCTING AND TESTING PROMPT TYPES

This section provides examples and information for implementing the prompt engineering concepts and topics presented in this chapter, including a Python script to build a prompt, a Jupyter notebook for testing and experimentation, the data used in the application, and a step-by-step guide for testing and validating the scripts.

Python Script

Example scripts (see Figure 2.1) for constructing and testing different prompt types in a simulated AI environment.

```
1   import openai
2   import os
3
4   # Set up your OpenAI API key
5   openai.api_key = os.getenv("OPENAI_API_KEY")
6
7   def generate_response(prompt, temperature=0.5, max_tokens=150):
8       """
9       Generates a response from the AI model given a prompt.
10
11      Parameters:
12          prompt (str): The input text prompt.
13          temperature (float): Sampling temperature. 1.0 makes the output more random, 0.0 makes it deterministic.
14          max_tokens (int): Maximum number of tokens to generate.
15
16      Returns:
17          str: The generated response text.
18      """
19      response = openai.Completion.create(
20          engine="davinci-codex",  # You can use other engines like "davinci", "curie", etc.
21          prompt=prompt,
22          temperature=temperature,
23          max_tokens=max_tokens,
24          n=1,
25          stop=None
26      )
27      return response.choices[0].text.strip()
28
29  def chain_of_thought_prompting():
30      prompt = (
31          "Solve the following math problem step-by-step:\n"
32          "Question: If you have 5 apples and you give away 3, how many do you have left?\n"
33          "Step 1: Identify the number of apples you start with.\n"
34          "Step 2: Identify the number of apples you give away.\n"
35          "Step 3: Subtract the number of apples given away from the number of apples you start with.\n"
36          "Step 4: State the final answer."
37      )
38      print("Chain-of-Thought Prompting Response:\n", generate_response(prompt))
```

FIGURE 2.1 Advanced prompt engineering techniques script.

Code Explanation: Advanced Prompt Engineering Techniques Script

This script demonstrates advanced prompt engineering techniques using the OpenAI API. The techniques include chain-of-thought prompting, self-consistency prompting, retrieval-augmented generation, prompt chaining, and tree of thoughts. Here's a detailed explanation tailored for learners interested in prompt engineering:

1. *Importing Libraries*

   The script begins by importing the "openai" library, which is essential for interacting with OpenAI's models. It also imports the "os" library to access environment variables securely.

2. *Setting Up the API Key*

   The API key is retrieved from an environment variable named "OPENAI_API_KEY". This approach is more secure than hard-coding the key directly in the script. It ensures that the key is kept confidential and not exposed in the codebase.

3. *Defining the "generate_response" Function*

   The "generate_response" function is defined to handle sending prompts to the OpenAI API and processing the responses. The function accepts a prompt as input, along with optional parameters for temperature (which controls the randomness of the response) and the maximum number of tokens (which limits the length of the response). Inside the function, a request is sent to the OpenAI API using the specified model, and the response is processed to return the generated text, stripped of any leading or trailing whitespace.

4. *Chain-of-Thought Prompting*

   This technique encourages the AI model to break down a problem into logical steps. In this script, the prompt guides the AI through a step-by-step process to solve a simple math problem, demonstrating how the model can be instructed to follow a structured approach to problem-solving.

5. *Self-Consistency Prompting*

   Self-consistency prompting ensures the AI provides consistent and logical answers by thinking through each step. The prompt in the script asks the AI to articulate its reasoning process step-by-step when answering a factual question. This technique is useful for tasks that require a logical flow of thought, such as answering questions that benefit from a structured reasoning process.

6. *Retrieval-Augmented Generation*

   Retrieval-augmented generation instructs the AI to consider external knowledge or the latest information when responding. The prompt in the script asks the AI to provide an up-to-date answer to a current affairs question, ensuring the response reflects the latest information.

7. *Prompt Chaining*

Prompt chaining involves building a sequence of prompts to refine and expand on the AI's responses. In the script, an initial prompt about the benefits of regular exercise is followed by a second prompt that asks for a detailed explanation of each benefit. This technique allows for more in-depth exploration of a topic by iteratively building on the AI's responses.

8. *Tree of Thoughts*

This technique involves asking the AI to plan or list out multiple possible options or steps for a given scenario. In the script, the prompt asks the AI to plan a weekend trip to Paris within a budget, listing possible activities, accommodation, and meals. This approach helps in generating comprehensive and organized responses for planning or brainstorming tasks.

Key Concepts for Prompt Engineering Learners

- *API Setup*: Understanding how to configure and use an API key to authenticate requests securely.
- *Function Creation*: Learning how to create and utilize functions to modularize code, making it reusable and easier to manage.
- *Advanced Prompt Techniques*: Exploring different prompting techniques to improve the quality and relevance of AI-generated responses.
- *Response Handling*: Learning how to process and clean up the AI's response to make it presentable and useful.

Datasets

Customer Interaction Data

A dataset of anonymized customer queries and AI responses, useful for analyzing prompt effectiveness.

Example from dataset:

```
[
  {
    "customer_query": "What is the current status of
my order #12345?",
```

```
    "ai_response": "Your order #12345 is currently
being processed and is expected to be shipped within
the next 24 hours."
  },
  {
    "customer_query": "Can you recommend a good hotel
in New York City for a family vacation?",
    "ai_response": "Sure! The Plaza Hotel and The
Peninsula New York are highly recommended for families
visiting New York City."
  },
  {
    "customer_query": "How can I reset my password?",
    "ai_response": "To reset your password, please
visit the 'Forgot Password' page on our website and
follow the instructions provided."
  },
  {
    "customer_query": "What are the best activities
for kids in San Francisco?",
    "ai_response": "Some of the best activities for kids
in San Francisco include visiting the Exploratorium,
the California Academy of Sciences, and riding the
cable cars."
```

CONCLUSION

This chapter has explored methodologies for developing effective prompts that align with the contextual requirements and desired outcomes of AI systems. The strategic design of prompts is instrumental in enhancing interactions between AI and users, influencing AI behavior, and optimizing response quality.

The efficacy of AI interactions is heavily reliant on the quality of the prompts it processes. When meticulously tailored to match specific situational contexts and the operational behavior of the AI system, these prompts significantly elevate the system's performance. An acute awareness of the comprehensive environment, user intent, relevant historical data, and specific tasks ensures that AI can finely tune its responses to align perfectly with the intricacies of the situation, enhancing both relevance and accuracy.

Understanding how an AI will respond under various circumstances is crucial, especially in environments where consistency and reliability are paramount, such as regulatory compliance or safety-critical operations. Crafting prompts that exploit the underlying algorithms and operational logic of the AI ensures predictable and stable outcomes, which builds user trust and compliance with standards.

Tailoring prompts to the specific needs and histories of individual users enhances the personalized nature of AI responses. Integrating data from previous interactions enables the AI to provide responses that anticipate user needs and preferences, which is crucial in domains such as e-commerce and personalized healthcare.

Clear and unambiguous instructions are the cornerstone of effective AI prompts. Concise, action-oriented language and avoidance of ambiguity are fundamental in creating interactions that are efficient, effective, and user-friendly. Incorporating feedback loops further enhances clarity and performance, ensuring that AI systems can request clarification when needed and adapt over time to better meet user needs.

Selecting the most effective prompt format is crucial for optimizing interactions between AI systems and users. Each format—whether cloze style, instruction-based, or hybrid—serves distinct purposes and dramatically influences the outcome of an AI's task execution and decision-making processes. Strategic application of different formats ensures that AI can handle a broader spectrum of tasks, improving its overall robustness and reliability.

The case studies presented in this chapter illustrate the practical application and impact of well-designed prompts in different AI scenarios. From financial services bots to university admission query assistants, these examples demonstrate how targeted changes to the prompt structure can significantly enhance AI functionality and user experience. By focusing on personalization, specificity, and context-awareness, AI applications achieve higher levels of precision and relevance in their interactions.

The exercises provided in this chapter aim to deepen your understanding of prompt engineering through practical experience. They focus on improving contextual sensitivity and clarity to ensure AI systems deliver more accurate and user-tailored responses. Developing these skills is crucial for improving the interactivity and user satisfaction of AI systems in real-world applications.

The chapter includes online supplemental materials, including code examples and datasets. . These resources provide additional support for constructing and testing different prompt types in simulated AI environments, analyzing prompt effectiveness, and exploring advanced concepts in prompt design.

By mastering the methodologies and techniques outlined in this chapter, developers and AI practitioners can ensure their systems operate not only with high efficiency but also with an attuned sense of context and user-centricity. This strategic approach to prompt engineering optimizes the functionality of AI systems and enhances the overall user experience, fostering more intuitive and responsive interaction landscapes.

PROMPTS AND CONTEXTUAL UNDERSTANDING

The ability of AI systems to understand and respond accurately to user inputs is crucial for effective interactions. Chapter 3 examines the pivotal role that prompts play in enhancing an AI's contextual comprehension, enabling it to deliver more relevant and precise responses. By leveraging advanced techniques in prompt design, developers can significantly improve the interaction quality between AI and users.

System messages are essential in shaping the AI's response patterns by establishing the conversational context and tone. These messages provide the necessary background and direction, guiding the AI to align its responses with user expectations and the specific situational requirements. Whether the tone needs to be formal, friendly, or professional, system messages ensure that the AI communicates appropriately, enhancing user engagement and satisfaction.

Explicit instructions are vital for ensuring that AI systems understand and execute tasks correctly. Clear and direct instructions reduce ambiguity, minimize misunderstandings, and enhance the efficiency of interactions. By providing detailed guidance, explicit instructions help AI systems perform tasks accurately, leading to smoother and more satisfying user experiences.

Enhancing prompts through augmentation techniques can significantly improve an AI's ability to understand and interact within various contexts. Techniques such as context enrichment, semantic expansion, and feedback incorporation enable AI systems to grasp the full scope of conversations, interpret user intentions more naturally, and continually refine their responses based on user feedback. These strategies are essential for developing AI that can engage in contextually rich and meaningful interactions.

The chapter also includes case studies that demonstrate the practical application of these concepts. For instance, an AI-driven tutoring system is enhanced to provide personalized guidance tailored to each student's learning pace and style, while a retail customer service bot is improved through emotion recognition and contextual backreferencing. These real-world examples highlight the transformative impact of advanced prompt engineering on AI performance and user satisfaction.

To solidify understanding, the chapter provides hands-on exercises focused on enhancing AI's contextual understanding and constructing dynamic prompts. These exercises offer practical experience in refining AI prompts, enabling developers to create more effective and responsive AI systems.

By mastering the principles and techniques discussed in this chapter, developers and AI practitioners can significantly elevate the performance of AI systems. The strategic use of prompts and contextual understanding not only optimizes AI functionality but also fosters more intuitive, engaging, and satisfactory interactions for users.

FUNCTION OF SYSTEM MESSAGES IN SETTING CONVERSATIONAL CONTEXT AND TONE

System messages are crucial in shaping the interaction between AI and users, playing a vital role in establishing the context and tone of a conversation. These messages guide the AI's response patterns to align with user expectations and the situational requirements, ensuring effective and meaningful exchanges.

Key Aspects

The following presents key aspects of setting conversational context and tone, including:

- Context Establishment
- Tone Setting

Context Establishment

System messages provide essential background information or set the scene for a dialogue, which helps the AI frame its responses appropriately. By establishing the context, system messages ensure that the AI understands the relevant details of the conversation, such as the user's needs, preferences, and the specific circumstances surrounding the interaction.

- Example

  In a customer service scenario, a system message might include information about the user's recent purchases or previous interactions with the company. This context allows the AI to offer more tailored and relevant assistance.

  - *Example System Message*

    "The user has recently purchased a laptop and has reported issues with the battery life. Address their concerns based on this information."

Tone Setting

The tone conveyed in system messages significantly influences how the AI's responses are perceived. Whether the desired tone is formal, friendly, or professional, it directly impacts user engagement and satisfaction. By setting an appropriate tone, system messages help create a consistent and coherent conversational experience that aligns with the brand's voice and user expectations.

- Example

  In a healthcare setting, a system message might adopt a compassionate and empathetic tone to make patients feel comfortable and understood.

  - *Example System Message*

    "The user is seeking advice on managing anxiety. Provide responses that are empathetic and supportive."

Detailed Exploration

The following is a detailed explanation of key aspects of setting conversational context and tone, including:

- Enhancing Context Awareness
- Influencing Response Style
- Improving User Experience

Enhancing Context Awareness

System messages can include specific instructions or details that enhance the AI's awareness of the context. This ensures that responses are not only relevant but also deeply informed by the user's situation and history.

▪ Example

For a financial advisory bot, a system message might include details about the user's investment history and risk preferences.

● *Example System Message*

"The user has a conservative risk profile and has recently invested in low-risk bonds. Provide investment advice that aligns with these preferences."

Influencing Response Style

The tone set by system messages influences the language style and formality of the AI's responses. This can vary depending on the application, from a casual and friendly tone in social media interactions to a formal and precise tone in legal or financial advice scenarios.

▪ Example

In a legal advice chatbot, a system message might enforce a formal tone to ensure the information provided is perceived as credible and authoritative.

● *Example System Message*

"The user is seeking legal advice on contract terms. Use a formal and precise tone in your responses."

Improving User Experience

By carefully designing system messages, developers can improve the overall user experience. Clear and contextually appropriate system messages help users feel understood and valued, leading to higher satisfaction and engagement.

▪ Example

In an e-commerce setting, a system message might aim to create a friendly and helpful atmosphere to encourage purchases.

- *Example System Message*

    "The user is browsing for holiday gifts. Use a friendly and enthusiastic tone to recommend popular gift items."

Case Study of an Application – Customer Service AI

Objective

Improve the customer service experience by refining system messages to better set the context and tone.

Challenge

Users felt that the AI responses were too generic and lacked a personal touch.

Solution

Implement system messages that include user-specific details and adopt a friendly, helpful tone.

- *Example System Message*

    "The user has contacted us about an issue with their recent order. Respond with a friendly and reassuring tone, offering solutions based on their order history."

Outcome

The enhanced system messages led to more personalized and engaging interactions, increasing user satisfaction by 25%.

By integrating these key aspects into the design of system messages, AI developers can significantly enhance the effectiveness of AI interactions. Establishing the right context and tone through system messages not only optimizes the functionality of AI systems but also fosters a more engaging and satisfying user experience.

IMPORTANCE OF EXPLICIT INSTRUCTIONS FOR EFFECTIVE AI GUIDANCE

Explicit instructions are essential for ensuring that AI systems understand and execute tasks correctly. By providing clear and direct instructions, the likelihood of errors is reduced, and the efficiency of interactions is significantly enhanced.

Significance of Explicit Instructions

The following section explains the significance of explicit instruction in prompt design, including:

- Clarity and Direction
- Reduced Misunderstandings
- Enhanced User Experience

Clarity and Direction

Explicit instructions provide clarity and direction, leaving little room for interpretation. This ensures that the AI processes requests accurately and performs tasks as intended. When instructions are clear, the AI can focus on delivering precise responses that meet user expectations.

- Example

In a technical support scenario, instead of asking, "Can you help with my computer issue?" an explicit instruction would be, "Please assist with troubleshooting the user's computer, specifically focusing on resolving the software installation error."

Reduced Misunderstandings

Explicit instructions minimize the risk of misunderstandings. By specifying the exact requirements and details of a task, the AI can deliver faster and more accurate responses. This reduction in ambiguity helps streamline the interaction process and enhances the reliability of the AI's performance.

- Example

For a booking system, rather than saying, "Book a flight," an explicit instruction would be, "Book a flight for the user from New York to Los Angeles on April 15th, departing in the morning and returning on April 20th in the evening."

Enhanced User Experience

Users benefit from a smoother interaction flow and experience less frustration when instructions are straightforward and concise. Clear instructions lead to a more intuitive and satisfying user experience, as the AI can respond effectively and efficiently to the user needs.

▪ Example

In an online shopping assistant, instead of a vague prompt like, "Help me find a dress," an explicit instruction would be, "Find a red evening dress in medium size, priced under $100, suitable for a formal event."

Detailed Exploration

The following section provides a detailed exploration of explicit instruction in effective prompt design, including:

▪ Precision in Task Execution

▪ Consistency in Responses

▪ User Confidence and Trust

Precision in Task Execution

Providing explicit instructions ensures that AI systems execute tasks with precision. This is particularly important in complex or multistep processes where each action must be performed correctly to achieve the desired outcome.

▪ Example

In a medical advice application, instead of a general prompt like, "Give health advice," an explicit instruction would be, "Provide advice on managing Type 2 diabetes, focusing on dietary recommendations and exercise routines."

Consistency in Responses

Explicit instructions help maintain consistency in AI responses. This is crucial in environments where consistent output is necessary, such as legal or financial services, where standardized information must be provided.

▪ Example

For a financial advisory bot, rather than asking, "What investment options are available?" an explicit instruction would be, "List the top three low-risk investment options for a user with a conservative risk profile, including expected returns and associated risks."

User Confidence and Trust

When AI systems consistently follow explicit instructions, it builds user confidence and trust. Users are more likely to rely on AI systems that deliver accurate and reliable results, knowing that their requests will be handled correctly.

■ Example

In a customer service setting, instead of a broad prompt like, "Handle the customer's complaint," an explicit instruction would be, "Address the customer's complaint about delayed shipping by offering a detailed explanation and potential compensation options."

Case Study of an Application – E-commerce Chatbot Enhancement

Objective

Enhance the e-commerce chatbot's performance by incorporating explicit instructions to improve task execution and user satisfaction.

Challenge

Users reported confusion and dissatisfaction with the chatbot's vague and unhelpful responses.

Solution

Implement explicit instructions in the chatbot's prompts to provide clear and direct guidance for resolving user queries.

■ Example Original Prompt
"Can I help you with something?"

■ Example Revised Prompt
"Please provide detailed assistance to the user regarding their recent order status, including expected delivery date and any tracking information."

Outcome

The introduction of explicit instructions led to a 30% increase in successful interactions and higher customer satisfaction ratings, as users received more precise and relevant responses.

By integrating explicit instructions into the design of AI prompts, developers can ensure that AI systems operate with greater accuracy, consistency, and user satisfaction. This strategic approach not only enhances the functionality of AI applications but also fosters a more efficient and enjoyable user experience.

PROMPT AUGMENTATION TECHNIQUES TO ENRICH AI'S CONTEXTUAL COMPREHENSION

Enhancing prompts through augmentation techniques can significantly improve an AI's ability to understand and interact within various contexts, making it more adaptable and intelligent. These techniques ensure that AI systems are not only responsive but also contextually aware, leading to more meaningful and effective interactions.

Augmentation Techniques

The following section presents augmentation techniques critical to contextual comprehension, including:

- Context Enrichment
- Semantic Expansion
- Feedback Incorporation

Context Enrichment

Adding situational details or relevant information to prompts helps the AI grasp the full scope of the conversation, leading to more appropriate and informed responses. By providing additional context, the AI can better understand the user's needs and the specific circumstances of the interaction.

- Example

  Instead of a general prompt like, "Give me the weather forecast," a context-enriched prompt would be, "Provide the weather forecast for Seattle for the next three days, focusing on temperature, chance of rain, and wind conditions, as the user is planning a hiking trip."

Semantic Expansion

Broadening the range of expressions and vocabulary used in prompts allows AI to better interpret user intentions and respond more naturally. This technique helps the AI understand a variety of ways users might phrase their queries, improving its ability to handle diverse inputs.

- Example

  For a travel booking system, rather than a simple prompt like, "Find flights," a semantically expanded prompt would be, "Search for available flights from New York to Paris, including options for economy and business class, considering flexible dates around mid-July."

Feedback Incorporation

Utilizing user feedback to refine prompts continually ensures that the AI remains aligned with user needs and expectations. By integrating feedback loops, developers can adjust and improve prompts based on real-world interactions, enhancing the AI's performance over time.

- Example

  In a customer support chatbot, instead of a static prompt like, "How can I help you?" a refined prompt based on feedback might be, "Please describe your issue in detail, including any error messages you've seen, so I can provide more accurate assistance."

Detailed Exploration

The following section provides detailed exploration of prompt augmentation techniques, including:

- Improving Contextual Awareness
- Enhancing Linguistic Flexibility
- Adapting Through Continuous Improvement

Improving Contextual Awareness

Context enrichment involves embedding relevant situational details within prompts to provide the AI with a comprehensive understanding of the interaction. This enables the AI to generate responses that are more aligned with the user's specific situation and needs.

- Example

  For a virtual health assistant, rather than a broad prompt like, "Give health advice," a context-enriched prompt could be, "Provide health advice for managing seasonal allergies, including tips on medication, lifestyle changes, and environmental factors, as the user has a history of severe reactions during spring."

Enhancing Linguistic Flexibility

Semantic expansion involves incorporating a wider range of vocabulary and expressions into prompts, allowing the AI to better recognize and respond to varied user inputs. This technique helps the AI understand nuances and subtleties in language, making interactions more natural and fluid.

▪ Example

In a restaurant recommendation bot, instead of a basic prompt like, "Find restaurants," a semantically expanded prompt could be, "Search for top-rated Italian restaurants in downtown Chicago that offer vegetarian options and outdoor seating."

Adapting Through Continuous Improvement

Feedback incorporation ensures that AI systems evolve based on user interactions. By regularly analyzing user feedback and adjusting prompts accordingly, developers can fine-tune the AI's responses to better meet user expectations and improve overall satisfaction.

▪ Example

For an online learning platform, rather than a generic prompt like, "What do you need help with?" a refined prompt based on feedback could be, "Please specify the topic or concept you're struggling with in your calculus course, so I can provide targeted explanations and practice problems."

Case Study Application – Enhancing an E-commerce Chatbot

Objective

Improve the e-commerce chatbot's ability to understand and respond to complex user queries by using prompt augmentation techniques.

Challenge

Users reported that the chatbot often provided irrelevant or incomplete responses due to a lack of contextual understanding.

Solution

Implement context enrichment, semantic expansion, and feedback incorporation to refine the chatbot's prompts.

▪ Example Original Prompt

"Can you help me with my order?"

▪ Example Context-Enriched Prompt

"Please provide details about your recent order, including the order number and any issues you're experiencing, so I can assist you more offectively."

▪ Example Semantically Expanded Prompt

"Describe the problem with your order, such as missing items, incorrect shipments, or delivery delays, so I can address your concerns accurately."

▪ Example Feedback-Incorporated Prompt

"Based on your previous feedback, please specify the exact issue with your latest purchase, including any error messages or discrepancies you've noticed."

Outcome

The augmented prompts led to a 40% increase in successful resolutions and higher user satisfaction rates, as the chatbot was able to provide more accurate and relevant assistance.

By incorporating these prompt augmentation techniques, developers can dramatically improve the AI's ability to understand and engage in contextually rich conversations. This approach not only enhances the overall effectiveness of the AI system but also elevates the user experience, making interactions more seamless and satisfactory.

CASE STUDIES

The following case studies are designed to provide additional context and detail related to the concepts and topics presented in this chapter. The case studies in this chapter are:

▪ Case Study 1 – AI Driven Tutoring System
▪ Case Study 2 – AI Customer Service Bot

Case Study 1 – AI-Driven Tutoring System

Objective

Enhance tutoring AI to provide context-sensitive guidance tailored to each student's learning pace and style.

Challenge

The initial system faced significant challenges in adapting its responses based on each student's historical performance and current learning context. This lack of adaptability led to generic responses that did not effectively address individual learning needs, resulting in lower engagement and suboptimal learning outcomes.

Solution

To overcome these challenges, a series of prompt augmentation techniques were implemented to integrate real-time data and historical learning patterns into the AI's responses. The goal was to create a more personalized and contextually aware tutoring experience.

Implementation Steps

Step 1 – Context Enrichment

- *Integration of Real-Time Data*

  The AI was equipped to utilize real-time data such as the student's current performance on tasks, time taken to complete exercises, and immediate feedback from quizzes.

- *Historical Learning Patterns*

  Incorporating data from past interactions, including previous scores, areas of difficulty, and topics mastered, allowed the AI to tailor its guidance more precisely.

Step 2 – Semantic Expansion

- *Diversified Vocabulary*

  The AI's prompts were enhanced with a broader range of expressions and vocabulary, allowing it to better understand and respond to varied student queries.

- *Adaptive Language*

  Depending on the student's proficiency and comfort level, the AI adjusted its language complexity, making it easier for students to understand and engage with the material.

Step 3 – Feedback Incorporation

- *Continuous Improvement*

  User feedback was continuously collected and analyzed to refine the prompts. This iterative process ensured that the AI remained aligned with student needs and could adapt to new learning trends.

- *Personalized Adjustments*

  Based on feedback, prompts were fine-tuned to address specific student concerns, such as offering more detailed explanations or providing additional practice problems for challenging topics.

Example Prompt Augmentations

- Before

  "What topic do you need help with?"

- After (Context Enriched)

  "Based on your recent quiz results, it looks like you might need help with algebra. Would you like to go through some practice problems on solving equations?"

- Before

  "How can I assist you today?"

- After (Semantic Expansion)

  "I noticed you've been working on geometry. Are there specific concepts like angles or triangles that you'd like more help with?"

- Before

  "Do you have any questions?"

- After (Feedback Incorporated)

  "Last time, you struggled with fractions. Shall we review some fraction problems together, or is there another topic you'd like to focus on?"

Outcome

The implementation of these prompt augmentation techniques led to significant improvements in the personalization of the tutoring process. Key outcomes included:

- Enhanced Personalization

  The AI could provide tailored guidance that matched each student's unique learning pace and style, making the learning experience more relevant and effective.

- Increased Student Engagement

  Students were more engaged and motivated to learn, as the AI's responses were directly aligned with their current needs and learning contexts.

- Improved Learning Outcomes

  There were measurable improvements in student performance, including higher test scores and better retention of material, as the AI could effectively address individual learning gaps.

- Positive Feedback

  Both students and educators reported higher satisfaction with the AI-driven tutoring system, appreciating its ability to provide personalized and contextually aware assistance.

This case study demonstrates the transformative impact of prompt augmentation techniques on AI-driven educational tools. By integrating real-time data, historical learning patterns, and user feedback, the AI system became more adept at delivering personalized and effective tutoring. These enhancements not only improved student engagement and learning outcomes but also highlighted the potential of advanced AI technologies in education.

Case Study 2 – Retail Customer Service Bot

Objective

Improve a retail bot's ability to handle a variety of customer interactions, including complaints and inquiries about products, with a focus on enhancing the personalization and relevance of responses.

Challenge

The initial bot responses were often generic and failed to address specific customer emotions or contexts. This lack of specificity and emotional intelligence led to customer frustration and decreased satisfaction, as the bot could not effectively respond to the nuances of each interaction.

Solution

To overcome these challenges, emotion recognition and contextual backreferencing were introduced in the bot's prompts. These enhancements aimed to tailor interactions based on the perceived customer mood and conversation history, thereby improving the bot's ability to provide relevant and empathetic responses.

Implementation Steps

Step 1 – Emotion Recognition

- *Sentiment Analysis Integration*

  The bot was equipped with sentiment analysis tools to detect customer emotions based on language cues. This allowed the bot to identify whether a customer was happy, frustrated, angry, or neutral.

- *Emotion-Specific Responses*

  Depending on the detected emotion, the bot adapted its responses to be more empathetic, apologetic, or celebratory, as appropriate.

Step 2 – Contextual Backreferencing

- *Conversation History Integration*

  The bot was programmed to reference previous interactions and transaction history, enabling it to provide more contextually relevant responses.

- *Personalized Prompts*

  Using the conversation history, the bot could tailor its responses to reflect the customer's past interactions and preferences.

Example Prompt Augmentations

- Before

  "How can I help you today?"

- After (Emotion Recognition)

  If Happy: "I'm glad to hear you're having a great day! How can I assist you with your shopping today?"

  If Frustrated: "I'm sorry to hear you're having issues. Let's get this sorted out for you as quickly as possible. Can you tell me more about the problem you're facing?"

- Before

  "Do you need help with an order?"

- After (Contextual Backreferencing)

  "I see you recently placed an order for a pair of running shoes. Are you inquiring about that order, or is there something else I can assist you with?"

- Before

  "What product are you interested in?"

- After (Combination of Techniques)

  "Based on your previous purchases, you might like our new collection of fitness gear. Would you like to hear more about our latest offerings, or do you need assistance with something specific?"

Outcome

The introduction of emotion recognition and contextual backreferencing led to significant improvements in the bot's performance. Key outcomes included:

- *Increased Customer Satisfaction Rates*

  Customers felt more understood and valued, leading to higher satisfaction rates. The bot's ability to respond empathetically to emotions played a crucial role in enhancing customer experiences.

- *Higher Resolution Rate at First Contact*

  By referencing previous interactions and providing contextually relevant information, the bot could resolve issues more effectively during the first contact, reducing the need for follow-ups.

- *Enhanced Engagement*

  Personalized interactions encouraged more meaningful engagement from customers, making them more likely to return and use the bot for future inquiries and purchases.

- *Positive Feedback*

  The improvements were reflected in positive customer feedback, with many users appreciating the bot's nuanced and empathetic approach to handling their queries and concerns.

This case study illustrates the powerful impact of integrating emotion recognition and contextual backreferencing into AI-driven customer service bots. By enhancing the bot's ability to understand and respond to customer emotions and contexts, businesses can significantly improve customer satisfaction and interaction outcomes. These advancements not only optimize the functionality of customer service bots but also foster deeper and more meaningful customer relationships.

TUTORIALS AND HANDS-ON EXERCISES

The following tutorials and hands-on exercises are designed to provide practical experience and application of the concepts and topics presented in this chapter. The tutorials and hands-on exercises in this chapter are:

- Exercise 1 – Enhancing AI's Contextual Understanding
- Exercise 2 – Dynamic Prompt Construction

Exercise 1 – Enhancing AI's Contextual Understanding

In this exercise, you will modify prompts used by a virtual event assistant to better understand and respond to varied user intents such as seeking event details, registering for an event, or providing feedback.

Steps

Step 1 – Identify Typical User Intents and Associated Contexts

- *Event Details*

  Users may inquire about the schedule, speakers, location, or agenda of the event.

- *Event Registration*

  Users may need assistance with signing up for the event, confirming their registration, or understanding the registration process.

- *Providing Feedback*

  Users may want to give feedback about their experience before, during, or after the event.

Step 2 – Create Augmented Prompts

Develop prompts that incorporate these contexts to guide AI responses effectively.

Examples

- *Event Details*

  "Can you provide details about the keynote speaker and the agenda for the event?"

▪ *Event Registration*

"I'd like to register for the upcoming conference. Can you guide me through the registration process?"

▪ *Providing Feedback*

"I have some feedback about the last session. How can I submit my comments?"

Step 3 – Simulate Interactions and Refine Prompts

Conduct simulations of various user interactions and refine the prompts based on the performance and accuracy of the AI's responses.

Simulation and Refinement Example

Scenario

A user asks, "What are the timings for the workshops?"

▪ Initial Prompt

"Provide workshop timings."

▪ Refined Prompt

"Can you provide the timings for the workshops scheduled on June 10th, including start and end times?"

Exercise 2 – Dynamic Prompt Construction

Exercise: Build Prompts for a Real Estate AI

In this exercise, you will build prompts for a real estate AI that adapts responses based on the user's interest level and prior interactions.

Steps

Step 1 – Design a Basic Prompt Template for Initial Interactions

Create a simple and generic prompt to initiate the conversation and gather initial information from the user.

▪ *Example Initial Prompt*

"Welcome to our real estate assistant. Are you looking to buy, rent, or sell a property?"

Step 2 – Develop Augmentation Strategies

Implement strategies to evolve the conversation based on user feedback and interaction history.

Examples

- User Interest Level

  "Based on your interest in waterfront properties, would you like to explore available listings in Miami Beach?"

- Prior Interactions

  "I see you previously inquired about 2-bedroom apartments. Here are some new listings that match your criteria."

Step 3 – Test and Analyze the Effectiveness of Dynamic Prompts

Conduct tests to analyze how well the dynamic prompts engage users and address their specific needs.

Testing Process

- Scenario 1

  A user expresses interest in luxury homes.

  - *Dynamic Prompt*

    "You mentioned an interest in luxury homes. Would you like to see properties with amenities like private pools and large gardens?"

- Scenario 2

  A user has previously asked about financing options.

  - *Dynamic Prompt*

    "Following up on your question about financing, would you like to connect with a mortgage advisor or explore properties within a specific budget range?"

Analysis and Refinement

- Collect user feedback and interaction data.
- Refine prompts to enhance clarity, relevance, and engagement.

By following these exercises, you can significantly improve the AI's contextual understanding and dynamic responsiveness, leading to more effective and satisfying user interactions. These practices help ensure that AI systems can adapt to diverse user intents and provide tailored, contextually relevant assistance.

PROMPTS IN PRACTICE

This section provides examples and information for implementing the prompt engineering concepts and topics presented in this chapter, including a Python script to build a prompt, the data used in the application, and a step-by-step guide for testing and validating the scripts.

Python Script

The following are sample scripts to illustrate how to implement context-aware prompt adjustments in Python (see Figure 3.1).

```python
# context_aware_prompt_adjustments.py >
1   def get_user_input():
2       # Function to simulate getting user input
3       return input("Enter a command: ")
4
5   def process_command(command):
6       # Function to process the user's command
7       if command.lower() == 'hello':
8           return "Hello! How can I help you today?"
9       elif command.lower() == 'goodbye':
10          return "Goodbye! Have a nice day."
11      else:
12          return "Sorry, I didn't understand that command."
13
14  def main():
15      while True:
16          user_input = get_user_input()
17          response = process_command(user_input)
18          print(response)
19
20          if user_input.lower() == 'exit':
21              break
22
23  if __name__ == "__main__":
24      main()
25
```

FIGURE 3.1 Basic command processing script.

Code Explanation: Basic Command Processing Script

This script demonstrates a basic command processing system using Python. It simulates a simple conversational interaction where the program responds to user inputs with predefined responses. The script includes functions for getting user input, processing commands, and controlling the flow of the interaction.

1. *"get_user_input" Function*

   This function simulates getting user input. It uses Python's "input" function to prompt the user to enter a command. The user's input is then returned as a string.

2. *"process_command" Function*

   The "process_command" function takes a command as its parameter and processes it to generate an appropriate response. The function converts the command to lowercase to ensure case-insensitivity. It then checks the command against predefined responses:

   • If the command is *"hello"*, it returns a greeting message.
   • If the command is *"goodbye"*, it returns a farewell message.

   For any other command, it returns a message indicating that the command was not understood.

3. *"main" Function*

   The "main" function controls the main flow of the script. It runs an infinite loop that:

   • Calls *"get_user_input"* to receive a command from the user.
   • Passes the command to *"process_command"* to get the corresponding response.
   • Prints the response to the console.

   The loop continues to run until the user inputs "exit", at which point the script breaks out of the loop and terminates.

4. *Script Execution*

   The script is designed to be executed directly. The condition *"if __name__ == "__main__":"* checks if the script is being run as the main module and, if so, calls the "main" function to start the interaction loop.

Key Concepts for Learners

■ *Input Handling:* Using the *"input"* function to capture user input in a Python script.

■ *String Manipulation:* Converting strings to lowercase to handle case-insensitive comparisons.

- *Conditional Logic:* Using if-elif-else statements to define different responses based on user input.
- *Loops:* Using a while loop to continuously prompt for user input until a specific condition is met (e.g., the user types "exit").
- *Function Modularity:* Breaking down the program into modular functions ("*get_user_input*", "*process_command*", "*main*") to make the code easier to understand and maintain.

Dataset

User Interaction Logs

A dataset featuring anonymized user interaction logs with an AI system, useful for developing and testing prompt adaptation strategies.

Example from dataset (see actual dataset on the companion site for this title for full data):

```
[
  {
    "user_id": "u001",
    "timestamp": "2024-06-01T10:15:30Z",
    "industry": "Healthcare",
    "interaction_type": "query",
    "user_input": "What are the symptoms of diabetes?",
    "ai_response": "Common symptoms of diabetes include
increased thirst, frequent urination, hunger, fatigue,
and blurred vision."
  },
  {
    "user_id": "u002",
    "timestamp": "2024-06-01T11:20:45Z",
    "industry": "Finance",
    "interaction_type": "query",
    "user_input": "What is the interest rate for a
savings account?",
    "ai_response": "The current interest rate for a
savings account is 1.5% annually."
```

CONCLUSION

Chapter 3 explored the essential role of prompts in enhancing the contextual understanding and response accuracy of AI systems. By implementing advanced techniques such as context enrichment, semantic expansion, and feedback incorporation, AI systems can significantly improve their ability to interact meaningfully and effectively with users.

Key Takeaways

- *The Function of System Messages*

  System messages play a critical role in setting the conversational context and tone, guiding AI responses to align with user expectations and situational requirements. These messages ensure that AI communications are appropriate, engaging, and effective.

- *Importance of Explicit Instructions*

  Providing clear and explicit instructions is vital for minimizing misunderstandings and ensuring accurate task execution. Detailed guidance helps AI systems perform tasks more efficiently, leading to smoother and more satisfying user interactions.

- *Prompt Augmentation Techniques*

  Techniques such as context enrichment, semantic expansion, and feedback incorporation are essential for enriching AI's contextual comprehension. These strategies enable AI to understand the full scope of conversations, interpret user intentions more naturally, and continually refine responses based on user feedback.

- *Real-World Applications and Case Studies*

  The case studies presented in this chapter, including the AI-driven tutoring system and the retail customer service bot, demonstrate the powerful impact of advanced prompt engineering. By integrating emotion recognition and contextual backreferencing, these systems have achieved higher levels of personalization, engagement, and user satisfaction.

The hands-on exercises have provided practical experience in refining AI prompts, focusing on enhancing contextual understanding and constructing dynamic prompts. These exercises are crucial for developing AI systems that are responsive, accurate, and user-friendly.

AI developers and practitioners can now significantly elevate the performance and effectiveness of AI systems. Strategic prompt engineering not only optimizes AI functionality but also fosters more intuitive, engaging, and satisfactory interactions for users. These advancements contribute to creating AI systems that are not only intelligent but also deeply responsive to the nuances of human communication.

As AI continues to evolve, the importance of sophisticated prompt design and contextual understanding will only grow. By focusing on these areas, developers can ensure that AI systems are equipped to meet the complex and diverse needs of users, driving better outcomes and fostering stronger, more meaningful interactions.

CHAPTER 4

FINE-TUNING PROMPTS
FOR SPECIFIC USE CASES

The effectiveness of AI systems hinges on their ability to understand and respond accurately to user inputs. Fine-tuning prompts is a critical aspect of this process, ensuring that AI systems can handle a wide range of specific use cases with precision and relevance. This chapter explores the methodologies and techniques for refining prompts to cater to diverse applications, enhancing the AI's performance and user satisfaction. Key topics covered in this chapter include:

- *Adapting Prompts to Different Domains by Integrating Specialized Knowledge*

Customizing prompts for specific domains by incorporating industry-specific terminology and knowledge.

Strategies for adapting prompts to align with the unique needs and language of various industries.

Examples from fields such as healthcare, finance, legal, and retail.

- *Ethical Considerations in Prompt Design, Focusing on Bias Mitigation*

Importance of ethical prompt design to ensure fair and unbiased AI interactions.

Techniques for identifying and mitigating biases in training data and prompt formulations.

Ensuring transparency and accountability in AI responses.

- *Iterative Process of Refining Prompts Through Evaluation and Testing*

The iterative nature of prompt refinement involves continuous testing and evaluation.

Steps in the iterative process, including initial testing, feedback collection, and prompt refinement.

Case studies demonstrating the impact of iterative refinement on AI performance.

Throughout the chapter, various real-world applications and case studies will be presented to illustrate the importance and impact of fine-tuning prompts for specific use cases. From legal assistance chatbots to marketing content generation tools, these examples will highlight how specialized prompt design enhances the functionality and effectiveness of AI systems.

To reinforce the concepts covered in this chapter, practical exercises will be provided. These hands-on activities will guide readers through the process of designing and refining prompts for different domains and use cases, ensuring they can apply these techniques in their own AI projects.

- Design prompts for a customer service AI operating in the telecommunications sector.
- Research common issues, create detailed scenario-specific prompts, test with simulated interactions, and refine based on feedback.
- Evaluate and revise prompts for an HR recruitment bot to ensure they are free from bias and ethically sound.
- Identify potential biases, redesign prompts to enhance fairness, conduct role-playing sessions, and test the effectiveness and ethical alignment.

This chapter emphasizes the ethical considerations in prompt design, focusing on bias mitigation and the importance of transparency and accountability. Discussions will include strategies for creating fair and unbiased prompts, ensuring that AI systems operate ethically and responsibly.

By the end of this chapter, readers will have a comprehensive understanding of how to fine-tune prompts for specific use cases. They will be equipped with the knowledge and tools needed to adapt prompts to various domains, mitigate biases, and iteratively refine prompts for optimal performance. This strategic approach to prompt design will enable the development of AI systems that are not only effective but also ethical and user-centric.

ADAPTING PROMPTS TO DIFFERENT DOMAINS BY INTEGRATING SPECIALIZED KNOWLEDGE

Customizing prompts for specific domains involves incorporating specialized knowledge that aligns with the needs and language of the industry or scenario. This approach ensures that AI systems can generate relevant and credible responses, effectively handle typical tasks or queries, and meet the expectations of stakeholders.

Strategies for Adaptation

This section includes strategies for adapting prompts using domain-specific knowledge, including:

- Industry-Specific Terminology
- Scenario-Based Customization
- Stakeholder Consultation

Industry-Specific Terminology

Using jargon and terms prevalent in a specific industry can help the AI generate more relevant and credible responses. Familiarity with industry-specific language enhances the AI's ability to understand and respond accurately to user queries, making interactions more seamless and efficient.

- Example in Healthcare

  Instead of a general prompt like, "Explain the procedure," an industry-specific prompt could be, "Can you explain the steps involved in a laparoscopic cholecystectomy?"

- Example in Finance

  Rather than asking, "What are the investment options?" an industry-specific prompt could be, "Can you provide information on high-yield bonds and their associated risks?"

Scenario-Based Customization

Tailoring prompts based on typical scenarios within the domain ensures that the AI can handle common tasks or queries effectively. By anticipating user needs and framing prompts to address specific situations, the AI can deliver more accurate and useful responses.

- Example in Retail

  For handling returns, a scenario-based prompt could be, "Please provide the process for returning an online purchase, including the necessary documentation and shipping instructions."

- Example in Education

  For providing homework help, a scenario-based prompt could be, "Explain the steps to solve a quadratic equation, including examples for better understanding."

Stakeholder Consultation

Engaging with industry experts and end users to refine prompt design can enhance the practical utility of the AI. By incorporating feedback from those who understand the nuances of the domain, the prompts can be adjusted to better meet real-world needs and expectations.

- Example in Manufacturing

  Consulting with engineers to develop prompts that help troubleshoot machinery issues, such as, "Describe the common causes of hydraulic system failures in CNC machines and suggest troubleshooting steps."

ETHICAL CONSIDERATIONS IN PROMPT DESIGN, FOCUSING ON BIAS MITIGATION

Ethical prompt design is crucial to ensure that AI systems operate fairly and do not perpetuate existing biases. By addressing key ethical considerations, developers can create AI that is equitable, transparent, and accountable.

Key Ethical Considerations

This section presents key ethical considerations, including:

- Bias Identification and Mitigation
- Transparency
- Accountability

Bias Identification and Mitigation

Actively identifying and mitigating biases in training data and prompt design is essential to prevent discriminatory outcomes. Biases can emerge from historical data, cultural stereotypes, or imbalanced datasets, leading to unfair treatment of certain groups. Strategies to address this include:

- Diverse Training Data

  Ensuring that training data is representative of different demographics and perspectives helps reduce the risk of bias.

- Bias Audits

  Regularly conducting audits to identify potential biases in AI responses and taking corrective measures to address them.

  Example Prompt Design

  Instead of a biased prompt like, "Suggest career options for women," a neutral prompt could be, "Suggest career options for individuals with a background in engineering."

Transparency

Designing prompts that ensure the AI's responses are understandable and traceable allows users to know how conclusions are reached. Transparency helps build trust in AI systems and allows for better user understanding and scrutiny.

- Explainability

  Creating prompts that lead to responses which include explanations of how decisions are made.

- Clear Instructions

  Ensuring that prompts are straightforward and the logic behind AI responses is easily comprehensible.

  Example Prompt Design

  "Provide a loan approval recommendation based on the applicant's credit score, income level, and debt-to-income ratio, and explain the factors influencing the decision."

Accountability

Establishing mechanisms to hold systems accountable for their outputs ensures adherence to ethical standards and regulations. Accountability involves setting up processes for monitoring, evaluating, and rectifying AI behaviors and outcomes.

* Regulatory Compliance

  Ensuring that AI systems comply with relevant laws and ethical guidelines.

* Feedback Loops

  Implementing feedback mechanisms where users can report issues or biases in AI responses, which are then addressed by the development team.

  Example Accountability Mechanism

  Providing a feedback prompt such as, "If you believe this response is biased or incorrect, please let us know for further review."

Detailed Exploration

This section provides detailed exploration of key ethical considerations, including:

* Mitigating Bias in AI Systems
* Ensuring Transparency
* Establishing Accountability

Mitigating Bias in AI Systems

Bias in AI systems can lead to unequal treatment and perpetuate existing societal inequalities. To mitigate bias, it is essential to do the following:

* Analyze Training Data

  Regularly review and update training datasets to ensure they are diverse and free from prejudices.

* Use Iterative Testing

  Continuously test AI systems in different scenarios to identify and rectify biased behaviors.

* Use Collaborative Development

  Involve diverse teams in the development process to bring multiple perspectives and reduce the risk of unconscious biases.

Ensuring Transparency

Transparency in AI systems ensures trust and allows users to understand and question AI decisions. To enhance transparency, do the following:

- Document AI Processes

  Clearly document how AI systems are trained, the data used, and the algorithms implemented.

- Offer User Education

  Provide users with information on how AI systems work and the rationale behind specific responses.

Establishing Accountability

Accountability ensures that AI systems are held to ethical standards and can be corrected if they deviate from these norms. Key actions include:

- Ethical Oversight

  Establish oversight committees to review AI performance and address ethical concerns.

- User Reporting Tools

  Develop tools that allow users to report suspicious or biased AI behavior, which can then be investigated and resolved.

Case Study of an Application – Financial Services AI

Objective

Ensure that a financial services AI provides fair and unbiased loan recommendations.

Challenge

Initial AI models exhibited bias against certain demographic groups due to historical data imbalances.

Solution

Implement bias mitigation strategies, enhance transparency, and establish accountability mechanisms.

- Example Original Prompt

  "Evaluate loan eligibility based on credit score."

■ Example Bias-Mitigation Prompt

"Evaluate loan eligibility based on credit score, income level, employment history, and provide a transparent explanation of the decision factors."

Outcome

The AI provided fairer loan recommendations, improved user trust, and complied with ethical and regulatory standards.

By incorporating these ethical considerations into prompt design, developers can create AI systems that are fair, transparent, and accountable. This approach not only enhances the functionality and reliability of AI but also ensures that these systems operate in a manner that respects and promotes equity and justice.

ITERATIVE PROCESS OF REFINING PROMPTS THROUGH EVALUATION AND TESTING

The process of refining prompts for AI systems is inherently iterative, requiring continuous testing and evaluation to adapt and improve the AI's performance. This approach ensures that AI systems can deliver precise, reliable, and contextually appropriate responses, remaining effective over time and adapting to new challenges and insights.

Steps in the Iterative Process

This section outlines the steps in the iterative process, which are as follows:

1. Initial Testing
2. Feedback Collection
3. Prompt Refinement

Step 1 – Initial Testing

The first step involves conducting initial tests to assess how well the AI understands and responds to the prompts. This phase is crucial for establishing a baseline of performance and identifying any immediate issues or areas where the AI may struggle.

■ Example

Deploying a new set of prompts for a customer service bot and monitoring its ability to handle common inquiries accurately.

- Objective

  Determine the initial effectiveness of the prompts and gather preliminary data on response accuracy and relevance.

Step 2 - Feedback Collection

After initial testing, feedback is gathered from users and stakeholders to identify specific areas for improvement. This feedback can provide valuable insights into how the AI's responses are perceived and highlight any gaps or shortcomings in the prompt design.

- Example

  Collecting user feedback on the clarity and usefulness of responses provided by an AI-driven virtual assistant.

- Objective

  Understand user experiences and pinpoint issues that need addressing to enhance the AI's performance.

Step 3 – Prompt Refinement

Based on the feedback and testing outcomes, adjustments are made to the prompts. This step involves analyzing the collected data, identifying patterns or recurring issues, and refining the prompts to address these challenges. The refined prompts are then retested, and the cycle continues until optimal performance is achieved.

- Example

  Modifying prompts to include more specific context or simplifying complex instructions based on user feedback.

- Objective

  Continuously improve the AI's ability to deliver precise and contextually appropriate responses.

Detailed Exploration

This section presents a detailed exploration of the iterative process:

- Importance of Iterative Testing
- Effective Prompt Refinement Techniques
- Collecting Comprehensive Feedback

Importance of Iterative Testing

Iterative testing is crucial for refining AI prompts because it allows for gradual and continuous improvement. Each iteration provides an opportunity to learn from previous mistakes, integrate new insights, and adapt to changing user needs or contexts.

- Example

  An AI customer support bot might initially struggle with understanding regional dialects or slang. Through iterative testing and refinement, prompts can be adjusted to improve comprehension and response accuracy.

Collecting Comprehensive Feedback

Gathering detailed feedback from a diverse group of users ensures that the prompt refinements are well-informed and address a broad range of scenarios. Feedback should be collected systematically, using tools like surveys, interviews, and direct user interactions.

- Example

  Implementing a feedback form at the end of each AI interaction, asking users to rate the helpfulness of the response and suggest improvements.

Effective Prompt Refinement Techniques

Effective refinement involves more than just minor tweaks; it requires a thoughtful analysis of the feedback and a strategic approach to implementing changes. Techniques such as A/B testing different prompt variations, analyzing response logs, and leveraging machine learning models to predict improvements can be employed.

- Example

  Using A/B testing to compare the effectiveness of different prompt structures and selecting the one that yields the best user satisfaction scores.

Case Study of an Application – Virtual Health Assistant

Objective
Enhance the virtual health assistant's ability to provide accurate and helpful medical advice.

Challenge

Initial prompts were too generic, leading to user dissatisfaction and frequent misinterpretations.

Solution

Implement an iterative process of testing, feedback collection, and refinement.

- *Example Initial Prompt*

  "What health advice do you need?"

- *Example Refined Prompt*

  "Please describe your symptoms, including any recent changes in your health, so I can provide more specific advice."

Outcome

Through iterative refinement, the virtual health assistant became more adept at understanding user queries and providing accurate advice, leading to higher user satisfaction and trust in the system.

The iterative process of refining prompts through evaluation and testing is essential for developing effective AI systems. By continuously testing, collecting feedback, and making informed adjustments, AI systems can be fine-tuned to deliver precise, reliable, and contextually appropriate responses. This ongoing cycle of improvement ensures that AI systems remain effective over time, adapting to new challenges and insights and enhancing the overall user experience.

CASE STUDIES

The following case studies are designed to provide additional context and detail related to the concepts and topics presented in this chapter. The case studies in this chapter are:

- Case Study 1 – Legal Assistance Chatbot
- Case Study 2 – Marketing Content Generation Tool

Case Study 1 – Legal Assistance Chatbot

Objective

Develop a legal assistance chatbot capable of providing personalized advice based on specific legal queries.

Challenge

The initial prompts used by the chatbot were too general, resulting in responses that lacked the necessary specificity and depth required for accurate legal advice. This led to user dissatisfaction and reduced trust in the chatbot's ability to provide meaningful assistance.

Solution

Customize the prompts by incorporating specialized legal knowledge and terminology relevant to various legal fields such as family law, corporate law, and civil rights. This involved:

- Industry-Specific Terminology

  Utilizing legal jargon and terms that are specific to different areas of law to ensure precise and contextually accurate responses.

- Scenario-Based Customization

  Creating prompts tailored to typical legal scenarios encountered within each legal field, ensuring the AI can handle common tasks or queries effectively.

- Stakeholder Consultation

  Engaging with legal experts and end users to refine prompt design and enhance the practical utility of the AI.

Example Prompt Refinements

- Before

  "How can I help you with your legal issue?"

- After (Family Law)

  "Are you seeking advice on divorce proceedings, child custody, or alimony arrangements?"

- After (Corporate Law)

  "Do you need assistance with contract drafting, business formation, or compliance with corporate regulations?"

- After (Civil Rights)

  "Are you looking for guidance on discrimination claims, rights violations, or legal protections?"

Outcome

The chatbot's ability to provide accurate and relevant legal advice significantly improved, leading to increased user trust and satisfaction. Users appreciated the specialized knowledge and tailored responses, which made the chatbot a more valuable resource for legal assistance.

Case Study 2 – Marketing Content Generation Tool

Objective

Enhance a content generation tool to produce marketing copy tailored to different industry sectors and target audiences.

Challenge

The generic responses generated by the tool failed to engage specific audience demographics, resulting in lower engagement and conversion rates.

Solution

Implement domain-specific prompts that integrate market trends, industry jargon, and audience preferences relevant to sectors such as technology, fashion, and healthcare. This involved:

* Context Enrichment

  Adding situational details and relevant market trends to prompts to make the generated content more aligned with industry standards and audience expectations.

* Semantic Expansion

  Broadening the range of expressions and vocabulary used by prompts to better capture the nuances of different industries and target demographics.

* Feedback Incorporation

  Utilizing feedback from marketing professionals and end users to continually refine and improve the prompts.

Example Prompt Refinements

* *Before*

  "Generate a marketing slogan."

- *After (Technology)*

  "Create a marketing slogan that highlights the cutting-edge innovation and reliability of our new AI-driven cybersecurity solution."

- *After (Fashion)*

  "Develop a catchy slogan that emphasizes the unique style and eco-friendly materials of our latest summer collection."

- *After (Healthcare)*

  "Write a persuasive marketing tagline that underscores the comprehensive care and patient-centered approach of our new telehealth services."

Outcome

The engagement rates on the generated content markedly improved, with increased conversion rates demonstrating the effectiveness of the tailored prompts. The content generation tool became more adept at producing industry-specific marketing copy that resonated with target audiences, enhancing overall marketing efforts and outcomes.

These case studies highlight the transformative impact of integrating specialized knowledge and industry-specific terminology into AI prompt design. By customizing prompts to align with the unique needs and language of different domains, AI systems can provide more accurate, relevant, and engaging responses. This approach not only enhances the functionality and effectiveness of AI applications but also significantly improves user satisfaction and trust.

TUTORIALS AND HANDS-ON EXERCISES

The following tutorials and hands-on exercises are designed to provide practical experience and application of the concepts and topics presented in this chapter. The tutorials and hands-on exercises in this chapter are:

- Exercise 1 – Domain Specific Prompt Design
- Exercise 2 – Ethics and Bias Mitigation in Prompts

Exercise 1 – Domain Specific Prompt Design

Objective

In this exercise, you will design prompts for a customer service AI specifically tailored to the telecommunications sector. This involves researching common issues, creating detailed scenario-specific prompts, and refining them based on simulated interactions.

Steps

Step 1 – Research Common Issues and Queries in Telecommunications

- Identify frequent customer service inquiries such as billing issues, network problems, plan upgrades, device troubleshooting, and account management.
- Gather data from customer service logs, forums, and telecommunications industry reports to understand the specific language and terminology used by customers.

Step 2 – Create Detailed, Scenario-Specific Prompts Addressing These Common Issues

- Develop prompts that are clear, specific, and directly address the identified issues.

Example Prompts

- *Billing Issues*

    "I see you have a question about your latest bill. Could you specify if the issue is related to an unexpected charge, payment not reflecting, or understanding the bill breakdown?"

- *Network Problems*

    "You mentioned a problem with your network connection. Is the issue with mobile data, Wi-Fi connectivity, or signal strength?"

- *Plan Upgrades*

    "Would you like to explore options for upgrading your current plan? We have new packages that include additional data and international calling."

- *Device Troubleshooting*
  "Please describe the issue you're facing with your device. Is it related to call quality, internet connectivity, or a specific app not working?"

Step 3 – Test the Prompts with Simulated Customer Interactions and Refine Based on Feedback

- Conduct simulations of customer interactions using the designed prompts to evaluate their effectiveness.
- Collect feedback from users and stakeholders on the clarity and relevance of the responses.
- Refine the prompts based on this feedback to improve accuracy and user satisfaction.

Example Refinement Process

- *Initial Prompt*
  "What is your billing issue?"

- *Refined Prompt*
  "I see you have a question about your latest bill. Could you specify if the issue is related to an unexpected charge, payment not reflecting, or understanding the bill breakdown?"

Exercise 2 – Ethics and Bias Mitigation in Prompts

Objective

In this exercise, you will evaluate and revise prompts for an HR recruitment bot to ensure they are free from bias and ethically sound. This process involves identifying potential biases, redesigning prompts, and testing them through role-playing sessions.

Steps

Step 1 – Identify Potential Biases in Current Prompt Formulations

- Review the existing prompts to identify language or structures that could lead to biased or unfair outcomes.
- Consider factors such as gender, race, age, and socioeconomic status that may be inadvertently impacted by the wording of prompts.

Example of Biased Prompt

"Do you have experience in managing a team of young professionals?"

Step 2 – Redesign the Prompts to Mitigate These Biases and Enhance Fairness

* Modify prompts to ensure they are inclusive and neutral, promoting fairness in the recruitment process.

Example of Revised Prompt

"Do you have experience in team management? Please describe the size and diversity of the teams you have managed."

Step 3 – Conduct Role-Playing Sessions to Test the Effectiveness and Ethical Alignment of the Revised Prompts

* Organize role-playing sessions where participants interact with the HR recruitment bot using the revised prompts.
* Collect feedback on the ethical alignment and effectiveness of the prompts from both participants and observers.
* Make further adjustments based on this feedback to ensure the prompts are fair, unbiased, and effective.

Example Role-Playing Session
Scenario
A candidate is asked about their leadership experience.

Initial Prompt
"How many years of experience do you have managing young teams?"

Revised Prompt
"Can you describe your leadership experience, including the types of teams you have managed and the challenges you have faced?"

By following these exercises, you can develop AI prompts that are not only domain-specific and effective but also ethically sound and free from bias. This approach ensures that AI systems can provide accurate, relevant, and fair responses, enhancing user satisfaction and trust.

PROMPTS IN PRACTICE

This section provides examples and information for implementing the prompt engineering concepts and topics presented in this chapter, including a Python script to build a prompt, the data used in the application, and a step-by-step guide for testing and validating the scripts.

Python Scripts

Scripts demonstrate how to incorporate domain expertise into AI prompts dynamically (see Figure 4.1).

```
def get_user_input():
    return input("Enter your query: ")

def process_query(query):
    if "hydraulic system" in query.lower():
        return ("Common causes of hydraulic system failures in CNC machines include low oil levels, leaks, "
                "and contamination. Suggested troubleshooting steps: Check the oil level and refill if necessary, "
                "inspect for leaks and repair as needed, and filter or replace the hydraulic fluid.")
    elif "electrical system" in query.lower():
        return ("Common causes of electrical system failures include short circuits, faulty wiring, and component wear. "
                "Suggested troubleshooting steps: Check for visible signs of damage or wear, test the wiring connections, "
                "and replace faulty components.")
    else:
        return "I can help with various machinery issues. Can you specify the system you're having trouble with?"

def main():
    while True:
        query = get_user_input()
        response = process_query(query)
        print(response)

        if query.lower() in ["exit", "quit"]:
            break

if __name__ == "__main__":
    main()
```

FIGURE 4.1 Fine-tuning prompts for specific domains.

Code Explanation: Fine-Tuning Prompts for Specific Domains

This script can be viewed through the lens of prompt engineering, particularly focusing on how prompts are crafted and fine-tuned to address specific domains such as hydraulic and electrical systems in machinery troubleshooting. Let's break down the code and relate it to prompt engineering principles.

1. *"get_user_input"* Function

   The "get_user_input" function captures user input. This function can be seen as the starting point where the user's prompt is collected. In prompt engineering, the quality and clarity of user input are crucial, as they set the context for the AI's response.

2. *"process_query"* Function

The "process_query" function processes the user's input (prompt) and generates an appropriate response based on specific keywords. This function demonstrates how prompts can be fine-tuned to provide domain-specific responses.

- *Keyword Detection*: The function checks if the user's query contains keywords like "hydraulic system" or "electrical system." This is akin to prompt engineering where specific keywords or phrases are used to trigger targeted responses.

- *Hydraulic System Prompt*: If the query mentions "hydraulic system," the function returns detailed troubleshooting steps specific to hydraulic system failures. This response is crafted to address common issues in this domain, such as low oil levels, leaks, and contamination. The suggested steps provide practical solutions, making the prompt both informative and actionable.

- *Electrical System Prompt*: If the query includes "electrical system," the function returns information on common electrical system failures like short circuits, faulty wiring, and component wear. The response includes troubleshooting steps to identify and fix these issues. This tailored prompt ensures that the response is relevant and useful for users facing electrical system problems.

- *General Prompt*: If the query does not contain specific keywords, the function prompts the user to provide more details about the system they are having trouble with. This general prompt helps guide the user to refine their query for more accurate assistance.

3. *"main"* Function

The "main" function runs an infinite loop, continuously prompting the user for input and processing their queries. This function demonstrates an iterative approach to prompt engineering, where the system continually refines its responses based on user input until a termination condition is met.

- *Iterative Refinement*: By repeatedly prompting the user, the system can gather more information and provide increasingly accurate responses. This mirrors the iterative nature of prompt engineering, where prompts are continuously fine-tuned based on feedback and results.

- *Exit Condition*: The loop breaks if the user inputs "exit" or "quit," providing a way to gracefully terminate the interaction. This shows the importance of having clear conditions to end the prompt interaction.

Key Concepts for Prompt Engineering

- *Domain-Specific Prompts*: Crafting prompts that are tailored to specific domains (hydraulic and electrical systems) ensures that responses are relevant and useful. This is crucial in prompt engineering to enhance the effectiveness of AI interactions.

- *Keyword Detection*: Using keywords to trigger specific responses helps in fine-tuning prompts to address particular issues accurately. This technique can be applied to various domains to improve response precision.

- *Iterative Refinement*: Continuously prompting the user and refining responses based on their input is a key aspect of prompt engineering. This iterative process helps in developing prompts that lead to more accurate and helpful AI outputs.

- *Guiding User Input*: Providing general prompts when specific information is lacking helps guide the user to refine their queries. This ensures that the AI can eventually generate a more accurate and targeted response.

Datasets

Industry Specific Interaction Data

Datasets containing anonymized interactions from various industries for training and testing prompts.

Example from dataset:

```
[
  {
    "user_id": "001",
    "timestamp": "2023-05-10T08:30:00",
    "interaction_type": "command",
    "user_input": "hello",
    "ai_response": "Hello! How can I assist you today?"
  },
```

CONCLUSION

Chapter 4 has explored the critical importance of fine-tuning prompts for specific use cases, highlighting how precise and contextually aware prompt design can significantly enhance the performance and reliability of AI systems. By integrating specialized knowledge, addressing ethical considerations, and embracing an iterative refinement process, developers can create AI systems that are both effective and responsible.

Key Takeaways

- *Adapting Prompts to Different Domains*

  Customizing prompts with industry-specific terminology and knowledge ensures that AI systems can provide accurate and relevant responses tailored to various fields. This domain-specific adaptation enhances the credibility and usefulness of AI interactions, making them more aligned with user needs and expectations.

- *Ethical Considerations in Prompt Design*

  Ethical prompt design is essential for preventing bias and ensuring fairness in AI responses. By actively identifying and mitigating biases, designing transparent and accountable prompts, and adhering to ethical standards, developers can build AI systems that operate justly and responsibly.

- *Iterative Refinement Process*

  The iterative process of refining prompts through continuous testing, feedback collection, and adjustments is vital for maintaining the effectiveness and accuracy of AI systems. This cycle of improvement allows AI to adapt to new challenges and insights, ensuring that it remains reliable and user-friendly over time.

- *Real-World Applications and Case Studies*

  The chapter has illustrated the practical applications of these concepts through real-world examples. From legal assistance chatbots providing accurate legal advice to marketing content generation tools producing engaging and industry-specific copy, the case studies demonstrate the transformative impact of fine-tuned prompts.

- *Hands-On Exercises*

  Practical exercises have provided readers with the opportunity to apply the techniques discussed in the chapter. By designing domain-specific prompts for a telecommunications customer service AI and revising HR recruitment bot prompts to mitigate bias, readers have gained hands-on experience in creating effective and ethical AI interactions.

- *Ethical Considerations*

  Throughout the chapter, the emphasis on ethical considerations has underscored the importance of building AI systems that are not only functional but also fair and accountable. Ensuring that AI operates without bias and with transparency is crucial for fostering trust and reliability.

By mastering the strategies and methodologies outlined in this chapter, developers and AI practitioners can significantly enhance the performance of their AI systems. Fine-tuning prompts for specific use cases ensures that AI interactions are precise, dependable, and contextually appropriate, leading to more effective and satisfying user experiences. Additionally, by prioritizing ethical considerations, developers can build AI systems that contribute positively to society, promoting fairness, transparency, and accountability.

This comprehensive approach to prompt design and refinement equips readers with the knowledge and tools needed to create AI systems that are not only powerful but also aligned with the highest standards of ethical and responsible AI development. As AI continues to evolve, these principles will remain foundational to building intelligent systems that serve and benefit all users equitably.

MONITORING AND EVALUATING PROMPT PERFORMANCE

In the evolving landscape of artificial intelligence, particularly in conversational AI, the effectiveness of prompts significantly influences user satisfaction and overall system performance. This chapter aims to establish robust strategies for assessing prompt effectiveness and enhancing AI interactions based on user feedback and real-world performance metrics.

IMPORTANCE AND IMPLEMENTATION OF EVALUATION METRICS SPECIFIC TO CONVERSATIONAL AI

Evaluation metrics are essential tools that help determine the effectiveness of AI prompts in real-world settings. These metrics provide quantifiable data that can be analyzed to assess how well an AI system performs, ensuring it meets the desired standards of accuracy, efficiency, and user satisfaction.

Key Metrics

- *Accuracy*

  Measures how often the AI's responses align with expected or correct outcomes. This metric is crucial for building trust and reliability in the AI system. High accuracy indicates that the AI can understand and respond correctly to user inputs, which is particularly important in applications where precise information is critical, such as legal advice or healthcare.

- Implementation

  Compare the AI's responses to a set of predefined correct answers or use expert evaluations to assess response accuracy.

- *Example*

  In a customer service bot, accuracy can be measured by checking how often the bot correctly resolves user issues based on historical data.

■ *Response Time*

Assesses the efficiency of the AI in delivering responses. In dynamic environments where quick interactions are essential, such as real-time customer support or emergency response systems, response time can significantly impact user satisfaction.

- Implementation

  Track the time taken from receiving a user query to delivering the AI's response.

- *Example*

  For a virtual assistant, response time can be measured by the average time it takes to answer user queries during peak and off-peak hours.

■ *User Satisfaction*

Gauged through surveys or direct feedback, this metric assesses how users feel about their interactions with the AI. This metric provides insights into the overall user experience and the perceived effectiveness of the AI system.

- Implementation

  Use post-interaction surveys, feedback forms, or sentiment analysis of user comments to gather data on user satisfaction.

- *Example*

  After each interaction with a chatbot, users might be asked to rate their experience on a scale of 1 to 5 and provide additional comments on their satisfaction.

■ *Engagement Rate*

Tracks how effectively the AI can keep users engaged over a conversation. This metric indicates the naturalness and relevance of the AI's responses, reflecting its ability to maintain meaningful and interactive dialogues.

- Implementation

  Monitor the length and depth of user interactions, including the number of turns taken in a conversation and the user's return rate for subsequent interactions.

- *Example*

  In an educational chatbot, engagement rate can be measured by the average session length and the number of follow-up questions asked by students.

Detailed Exploration

This section provides detailed exploration of key metrics for conversational AI, including:

- Ensuring Accuracy
- Optimizing Response Time
- Enhancing User Satisfaction

Ensuring Accuracy

High accuracy is achieved through rigorous training and continual refinement of the AI system. Regularly updating the training data and employing techniques such as supervised learning can help maintain high accuracy levels.

Example

A financial advisory bot might use updated market data and feedback from financial experts to ensure that its investment recommendations remain accurate and relevant.

Optimizing Response Time

Optimizing response time involves streamlining the AI's processing capabilities and ensuring that the underlying infrastructure supports rapid data handling and response generation.

Example

Implementing faster algorithms and improving server response times can help a telehealth AI system deliver timely medical advice, which is crucial in urgent care situations.

Enhancing User Satisfaction

Enhancing user satisfaction requires understanding user needs and preferences, which can be achieved through regular feedback and adaptive learning techniques that personalize the AI's responses.

Example

A virtual shopping assistant might use user feedback to refine its product recommendations, ensuring they align with individual preferences and improving overall satisfaction.

Boosting Engagement Rates

Boosting engagement rates involves creating more natural and contextually aware interactions. Techniques such as natural language understanding (NLU) and context retention can help the AI maintain engaging and relevant dialogues.

Example

An educational chatbot that remembers a student's previous questions and learning progress can provide more tailored and engaging educational content, encouraging longer and more meaningful interactions.

Case Study of an Application – Enhancing a Customer Service Chatbot

Objective

Improve the performance and user satisfaction of a customer service chatbot through effective evaluation metrics.

Metrics Implemented

- Accuracy
  Ensured correct resolution of customer issues.

- Response Time
  Reduced the average response time to under two seconds.

- User Satisfaction
  Collected user ratings after each interaction, aiming for an average rating of 4.5 out of 5.

- Engagement Rate
  Increased the average conversation length and user return rate.

Outcome

The customer service chatbot saw a 20% increase in user satisfaction scores, a 15% reduction in average response time, and a 25% improvement in engagement rates, demonstrating the effectiveness of using targeted evaluation metrics to drive improvements.

By systematically implementing and monitoring these evaluation metrics, developers can ensure their conversational AI systems are accurate, efficient, engaging, and satisfying for users. This strategic approach to evaluation not only enhances the performance of AI systems but also fosters trust and reliability, crucial for long-term user adoption and success.

In the following sections, we will delve into various implementation strategies, methods for collecting and utilizing user feedback, and analyzing real-world interactions to continually refine and optimize AI prompts. By adopting these strategies, developers can create AI systems that are responsive, dependable, and user-centered, ensuring sustained engagement and satisfaction.

IMPORTANCE AND IMPLEMENTATION OF EVALUATION METRICS SPECIFIC TO CONVERSATIONAL AI

Evaluation metrics are essential tools that help determine the effectiveness of AI prompts in real-world settings, guiding continuous improvements and optimizations. These metrics provide quantifiable data that can be analyzed to assess how well an AI system performs, ensuring it meets the desired standards of accuracy, efficiency, and user satisfaction.

Key Metrics

This section provides information on key metrics for enhancing performance and customer service, including:

- Accuracy
- Response Time
- User Satisfaction
- Engagement Rate

Accuracy

Accuracy measures how often the AI's responses align with expected or correct outcomes. This metric is crucial for building trust and reliability in the AI system. High accuracy indicates that the AI can understand

and respond correctly to user inputs, which is particularly important in applications where precise information is critical, such as legal advice or healthcare.

Implementation

- Compare the AI's responses to a set of predefined correct answers or use expert evaluations to assess response accuracy.

Example

- In a customer service bot, accuracy can be measured by checking how often the bot correctly resolves user issues based on historical data.

Response Time

Response time assesses the efficiency of the AI in delivering responses. In dynamic environments where quick interactions are essential, such as real-time customer support or emergency response systems, response time can significantly impact user satisfaction.

Implementation

- Track the time taken from receiving a user query to delivering the AI's response.

Example

- For a virtual assistant, response time can be measured by the average time it takes to answer user queries during peak and off-peak hours.

User Satisfaction

User satisfaction is gauged through surveys or direct feedback and assesses how users feel about their interactions with the AI. This metric provides insights into the overall user experience and the perceived effectiveness of the AI system.

Implementation

- Use post interaction surveys, feedback forms, or sentiment analysis of user comments to gather data on user satisfaction.

Example

- After each interaction with a chatbot, users might be asked to rate their experience on a scale of 1 to 5 and provide additional comments on their satisfaction.

Engagement Rate

Engagement rate tracks how effectively the AI can keep users engaged over a conversation. This metric indicates the naturalness and relevance of the AI's responses, reflecting its ability to maintain meaningful and interactive dialogues.

Implementation

- Monitor the length and depth of user interactions, including the number of turns taken in a conversation and the user's return rate for subsequent interactions.

Example

- In an educational chatbot, engagement rate can be measured by the average session length and the number of follow-up questions asked by students.

Detailed Exploration

This section provides detailed exploration of enhancing performance and customer service, including:

- Ensuring Accuracy
- Optimizing Response Time
- Enhancing User Satisfaction
- Boosting Engagement Rates

Ensuring Accuracy

High accuracy is achieved through rigorous training and continual refinement of the AI system. Regularly updating the training data and employing techniques such as supervised learning can help maintain high accuracy levels.

Example

A financial advisory bot might use updated market data and feedback from financial experts to ensure that its investment recommendations remain accurate and relevant.

Optimizing Response Time

Optimizing response time involves streamlining the AI's processing capabilities and ensuring that the underlying infrastructure supports rapid data handling and response generation.

Example

Implementing faster algorithms and improving server response times can help a telehealth AI system deliver timely medical advice, which is crucial in urgent care situations.

Enhancing User Satisfaction

Enhancing user satisfaction requires understanding user needs and preferences, which can be achieved through regular feedback and adaptive learning techniques that personalize the AI's responses.

Example

A virtual shopping assistant might use user feedback to refine its product recommendations, ensuring they align with individual preferences and improving overall satisfaction.

Boosting Engagement Rates

Boosting engagement rates involves creating more natural and contextually aware interactions. Techniques such as NLU and context retention can help the AI maintain engaging and relevant dialogues.

Example

An educational chatbot that remembers a student's previous questions and learning progress can provide more tailored and engaging educational content, encouraging longer and more meaningful interactions.

Case Study Application – Enhancing a Customer Service Chatbot

Objective

Improve the performance and user satisfaction of a customer service chatbot through effective evaluation metrics.

Metrics Implemented

- Accuracy
  Ensured correct resolution of customer issues.

- Response Time
  Reduced the average response time to under two seconds.

- User Satisfaction

  Collected user ratings after each interaction, aiming for an average rating of 4.5 out of 5.

- Engagement Rate

  Increased the average conversation length and user return rate.

Outcome

The customer service chatbot saw a 20% increase in user satisfaction scores, a 15% reduction in average response time, and a 25% improvement in engagement rates, demonstrating the effectiveness of using targeted evaluation metrics to drive improvements.

By systematically implementing and monitoring these evaluation metrics, developers can ensure their conversational AI systems are accurate, efficient, engaging, and satisfying for users. This strategic approach to evaluation not only enhances the performance of AI systems but also fosters trust and reliability, crucial for long-term user adoption and success.

IMPLEMENTATION STRATEGIES

Effectively implementing evaluation metrics and refining prompts for conversational AI systems requires a systematic approach. Key strategies include automated testing and A/B testing, both of which provide valuable data to guide improvements and optimizations.

Automated Testing

Automated testing involves using scripts and AI tools to simulate various scenarios and measure performance across different metrics. This method allows for consistent and repeatable testing conditions, ensuring that the AI's performance is evaluated accurately and efficiently.

Key Steps in Automated Testing

Step 1 – Scenario Simulation

- Develop scripts that simulate a wide range of user interactions, including common queries, edge cases, and complex scenarios.
- Use these scripts to test the AI's responses under controlled conditions.

Step 2 – Metric Measurement

- Automatically measure key metrics such as accuracy, response time, user satisfaction, and engagement rate during each simulation.
- Record and analyze data to identify patterns and areas for improvement.

Step 3 – Continuous Integration

- Integrate automated testing into the development pipeline to regularly assess the AI's performance.
- Use continuous testing to detect issues early and ensure that updates do not degrade the system's performance.

Example: Application Customer Service Chatbot

- Scripts simulate various customer inquiries such as billing issues, technical support, and service complaints.
- Automated tools measure response accuracy, speed, and user satisfaction.
- Continuous integration ensures that each new update maintains or improves the chatbot's performance.

A/B Testing

A/B testing compares different versions of prompts to determine which performs better under the same conditions. This data-driven approach allows for informed refinements and optimizations based on user interactions and feedback.

Key Steps in A/B Testing

Step 1 – Version Creation

- Develop multiple versions of prompts that address the same user queries but with variations in language, structure, or context.
- Ensure that each version is designed to test specific hypotheses about prompt effectiveness.

Step 2 – User Segmentation

- Randomly assign users to distinct groups, with each group interacting with a different version of the prompts.

▪ Ensure a representative sample to obtain reliable and generalizable results.

Step 3 – Performance Measurement

▪ Measure performance across key metrics such as accuracy, response time, user satisfaction, and engagement rate for each version.

▪ Use statistical analysis to compare results and determine which version performs best.

Step 4 – Data-Driven Refinement

▪ Analyze the data to identify which prompt versions lead to better outcomes.

▪ Implement the best performing prompts and continue the testing cycle to refine further.

Example: Application Educational AI Tutor

▪ Two versions of a prompt for explaining a mathematical concept are created.

▪ One group of students receives version A, while another group receives version B.

▪ Performance metrics such as comprehension rates, engagement, and satisfaction are measured.

▪ Data analysis reveals that version B leads to higher comprehension and satisfaction, so it is adopted and further refined.

Combining Strategies for Optimal Results

Combining automated testing and A/B testing provides a comprehensive approach to evaluating and refining AI prompts. Automated testing ensures that the AI system performs well across a wide range of scenarios, while A/B testing provides detailed insights into the effectiveness of specific prompt variations.

Example: Combined Approach Healthcare Virtual Assistant

Automated Testing

Scripts simulate patient inquiries about symptoms, medications, and appointments to measure accuracy and response time.

A/B Testing

Different versions of prompts for symptom checking are tested to determine which version provides clearer and more helpful responses.

Outcome

The combined approach identifies high-performing prompts that improve patient satisfaction and ensure timely, accurate assistance.

By leveraging automated testing and A/B testing, developers can systematically improve the performance and user experience of conversational AI systems. These implementation strategies enable continuous refinement and optimization, ensuring that AI systems remain effective, efficient, and user-friendly over time.

METHODS FOR COLLECTING AND UTILIZING USER FEEDBACK TO REFINE PROMPTS

User feedback is invaluable for continuously improving the relevance and effectiveness of AI prompts. By systematically collecting and analyzing feedback, developers can make targeted adjustments to enhance the performance of AI systems.

Collection Methods

The following collection methods are used to systematically collect and analyze feedback, including:

- Interactive Surveys
- Feedback Buttons
- User Interviews

Interactive Surveys

Embedding short surveys within AI interactions allows for immediate, context-specific feedback. This method captures users' thoughts and experiences in real time, providing accurate and relevant insights.

- *Implementation*
  Include a brief survey at the end of an interaction asking users to rate their experience or provide comments.

Use multiple choice questions, star ratings, or open-ended text fields to gather diverse types of feedback.

- Example

  After a chatbot helps a customer resolve an issue, a survey might ask, "How satisfied are you with the assistance you received?" with options ranging from 1 to 5 stars.

Feedback Buttons

Providing users with an easy way to rate responses or report issues directly through the interaction interface encourages ongoing feedback without interrupting the user experience.

- Implementation
  - Integrate thumbs up/thumbs down buttons, star ratings, or feedback icons within the chat interface.
  - Allow users to click these buttons to indicate their satisfaction or to flag responses that were unhelpful or incorrect.

    - Example

      During an interaction, users can click a thumbs up or thumbs down button next to the chatbot's response to indicate whether the answer was helpful.

User Interviews

Conducting detailed discussions with frequent users provides deeper insights into their experiences and suggestions. This qualitative method helps uncover nuanced feedback that surveys might miss.

- Implementation
  - Schedule regular interviews with a diverse group of frequent users to discuss their interactions with the AI.
  - Use structured or semistructured interview formats to explore specific aspects of their experiences.

    - Example

      An AI development team might conduct monthly interviews with power users of a virtual assistant to gather detailed feedback on how well the AI meets their needs.

Utilization Strategies

This section provides information on utilization strategies, including:

- Feedback Analysis
- Iterative Feedback

Feedback Analysis

Regularly reviewing feedback to identify common issues or suggestions is crucial for understanding user needs and improving prompt design. Analyzing feedback helps pinpoint recurring problems and areas for enhancement.

Implementation

- Aggregate feedback from various sources and categorize it by theme or issue.
- Use data analytics tools to detect patterns and trends in user feedback.
  - Example
    Analyzing feedback from surveys and feedback buttons might reveal that users frequently report issues with the AI's ability to understand specific technical jargon.

Iterative Refinement

Applying insights from user feedback to make targeted adjustments to prompts, then retesting to assess impact, is essential for continuous improvement. This iterative process ensures that changes lead to tangible enhancements in AI performance.

Implementation

- Use feedback analysis to inform specific changes in prompt wording, structure, or context.
- Implement the changes and conduct A/B testing or automated testing to evaluate their effectiveness.
  - Example
    - If feedback indicates confusion about certain prompts, the AI team might rephrase those prompts for clarity, then use A/B testing to determine if the new versions improve user understanding and satisfaction.

Case Study of an Application – Improving a Customer Support Chatbot

Objective

Enhance the chatbot's ability to provide accurate and relevant support based on user feedback.

Collection Methods

- Interactive Surveys

  Users are asked to rate their satisfaction after each interaction.

- Feedback Buttons

  Thumbs up and thumbs down buttons are integrated into the chat interface.

- User Interviews

  Monthly interviews are conducted with frequent users to gather detailed insights.

Utilization Strategies

- Feedback Analysis

  Regular review of survey results and feedback button data identifies common issues with specific types of queries.

- Iterative Refinement

  Insights from feedback indicate that users often find billing-related responses confusing. The prompts are revised for clarity, and A/B testing shows a significant increase in user satisfaction with billing queries.

Outcome

The systematic collection and utilization of user feedback led to a 30% improvement in overall user satisfaction, demonstrating the value of feedback-driven refinement in enhancing AI performance.

By implementing these methods for collecting and utilizing user feedback, developers can ensure their AI systems continuously evolve to meet user needs more effectively. This approach not only improves the accuracy and relevance of AI responses but also fosters greater user trust and satisfaction.

ANALYZING REAL-WORLD INTERACTIONS TO IDENTIFY IMPROVEMENTS AND ADJUSTMENTS IN PROMPT DESIGN

Real-world interaction analysis involves studying how AI prompts perform under various real-life conditions to fine-tune their effectiveness. By evaluating actual user interactions, developers can identify necessary adjustments to enhance the AI's performance and ensure it meets user needs more accurately.

Analysis Techniques

The following analysis techniques may be used to determine AI performance and user satisfaction, including:

- Conversation Logs
- Contextual Performance
- Longitudinal Studies

Conversation Logs

Analyzing conversation logs helps identify patterns, failures, or successes in AI interactions. By reviewing these logs, developers can pinpoint specific instances where the AI either performed exceptionally well or struggled, allowing for targeted improvements.

Implementation

- Collect and review logs of user interactions over a specified period.
- Look for recurring issues, misunderstandings, or successful engagements.
- Categorize interactions based on the type of query, user sentiment, and outcome.
  - Example
    - Analyzing logs from a customer service chatbot might reveal that users frequently misunderstand prompts related to account management, suggesting a need for clearer instructions.

Contextual Performance

Evaluating how well prompts manage different contextual scenarios involves assessing the AI's ability to respond accurately and appropriately across various contexts. This analysis helps identify areas where additional information or clarity might enhance performance.

Implementation

- Test prompts across a range of scenarios, including edge cases and common queries.
- Assess how well the AI adapts its responses based on contextual cues and user inputs.
- Identify scenarios where the AI's performance could be improved with more specific or detailed prompts.
  - Example
    - A virtual health assistant might be tested on its ability to provide dietary advice to users with different health conditions. Analysis might show that prompts need to be more specific about dietary restrictions for users with diabetes.

Longitudinal Studies

Monitoring prompt performance over extended periods helps understand how changes affect long-term user engagement and satisfaction. Longitudinal studies provide insights into the sustainability and long-term impact of prompt adjustments.

Implementation

- Track the performance of specific prompts over several months.
- Measure key metrics such as user satisfaction, engagement rates, and accuracy over time.
- Compare performance data before and after implementing changes to evaluate their effectiveness.
  - Example
    - A study on an educational chatbot might track how students' engagement and comprehension rates change over a semester as prompts are refined to provide clearer explanations and more relevant examples.

Comprehensive Framework for Monitoring and Evaluating AI Prompts

By focusing on these areas, this chapter provides a comprehensive framework for monitoring and evaluating the effectiveness of AI prompts. This approach ensures continuous improvement and user-centered design, enhancing the performance and reliability of AI systems, including:

- *Collecting Data*
  - Use conversation logs, contextual performance assessments, and longitudinal studies to gather detailed data on AI interactions.
  - Ensure data collection methods are robust and comprehensive, covering a wide range of user interactions.

- *Identifying Patterns*
  - Analyze the collected data to identify patterns of success and failure in AI responses.
  - Categorize issues based on frequency, severity, and impact on user satisfaction.

- *Adjusting*
  - Use insights from data analysis to make targeted adjustments to prompts.
  - Focus on areas where clarity, context, or specificity can improve AI performance.

- *Testing Changes*
  - Implement changes and use automated testing, A/B testing, and user feedback to evaluate their impact.
  - Ensure that changes lead to measurable improvements in key metrics.

- *Continuous Monitoring*
  - Regularly monitor AI performance to detect new issues and opportunities for further refinement.
  - Maintain an iterative process of testing, feedback collection, and prompt adjustment.

Case Study of an Application – Enhancing a Customer Support Chatbot

Objective

Improve the chatbot's ability to manage complex customer queries effectively.

Analysis Techniques

- Conversation Logs
  Analyzed logs to identify common points of failure in handling billing inquiries.

- Contextual Performance

  Tested the chatbot's responses in various billing scenarios, such as past due payments and disputed charges.

- Longitudinal Studies

  Monitored user satisfaction and resolution rates over six months to assess the impact of prompt changes.

Outcome

- Identified that prompts related to billing disputes were often misunderstood.

- Refined these prompts to include more detailed explanations and step-by-step guidance.

- Achieved a 25% increase in resolution rates and a 20% improvement in user satisfaction over six months.

By implementing these analysis techniques and focusing on real-world interactions, developers can ensure that AI prompts are continually refined to meet user needs effectively. This comprehensive framework supports the development of AI systems that are responsive, dependable, and user centered, fostering long-term engagement and satisfaction.

CASE STUDIES

The following case studies are designed to provide additional context and detail related to the concepts and topics presented in this chapter. The case studies in this chapter are:

- Case Study 1 – Customer Support Analysis
- Case Study 2 – Educational Bot Effectiveness

Case Study 1 – Customer Support Analysis

Objective

Improve the performance of a customer support AI by closely monitoring and adjusting prompts based on real-world interactions.

Challenge

Initial response metrics indicated low customer satisfaction and high escalation rates. Customers often felt that the AI's responses were unclear or irrelevant, leading to frustration and frequent handoffs to human agents.

Solution

Implement a system for continuous monitoring of interaction metrics and adjust prompts accordingly to improve clarity and relevance. This involved:

- *Continuous Monitoring*

  Analyzed conversation logs to identify recurring issues and patterns in customer queries.

  Monitored key metrics such as customer satisfaction scores, response times, and escalation rates.

- *Dynamic Prompt Adjustments*

  Refined prompts to address common issues identified through conversation logs.

  Introduced more context-specific prompts to ensure the AI's responses were relevant and clear.

  Conducted A/B testing to evaluate the effectiveness of different prompt variations.

- *Iterative Refinement*

  Used customer feedback from interactive surveys and feedback buttons to continually improve prompts.

  Conducted regular reviews and adjustments to keep prompts aligned with evolving customer needs and expectations.

Outcome

The continuous monitoring and dynamic prompt adjustments led to a significant improvement in the AI's performance. Customer satisfaction increased by 30%, and the need for human escalation was reduced by 25%. These results demonstrated the effectiveness of using real-world interaction analysis to enhance prompt design.

Case Study 2 – Educational Bot Effectiveness

Objective

Enhance an educational bot to better assist students with homework and learning activities.

Challenge

Students reported that the bot often misunderstood their questions or provided irrelevant information. This led to frustration and reduced engagement with the bot as a learning tool.

Solution

Deploy a structured evaluation framework to monitor bot interactions, identify misunderstandings, and refine prompts for better contextual alignment. This involved:

- *Structured Evaluation Framework*

  Implemented a system for logging and analyzing all student interactions.

  Used these logs to identify common misunderstandings and irrelevant responses.

- *Prompt Refinement*

  Refined prompts to improve the bot's ability to understand and respond to student queries accurately.

  Introduced more detailed and contextually aware prompts based on the specific subject matter and common student questions.

- *User Feedback Integration*

  Conducted surveys and user interviews to gather detailed feedback from students and educators.

  Used this feedback to make targeted adjustments to the bot's prompts and responses.

- *Iterative Testing and Improvement*

  Continuously tested the refined prompts in real-world classroom settings.

  Analyzed performance metrics such as student engagement, accuracy of responses, and user satisfaction.

Outcome

The educational bot showed a marked improvement in its ability to comprehend student queries and provide relevant assistance. The rate of correct assistance increased by 40%, and positive feedback from both students and educators highlighted the bot's enhanced effectiveness as a learning tool. This case study underscores the importance of a structured and iterative approach to prompt refinement in improving AI performance in educational settings.

These case studies illustrate the powerful impact of analyzing real-world interactions and dynamically adjusting prompts to enhance AI performance. By implementing continuous monitoring, structured evaluation frameworks, and iterative refinement processes, AI systems can be made more responsive, accurate, and user-friendly. This approach not only improves immediate user satisfaction and engagement but also ensures that AI systems remain effective and relevant over time.

TUTORIALS AND HANDS-ON EXERCISES

The following tutorials and hands-on exercises are designed to provide practical experience and application of the concepts and topics presented in this chapter. The tutorials and hands-on exercises in this chapter are:

- Exercise 1 – Setting Up Monitoring Systems
- Exercise 2 – Analyzing and Refining AI Prompts

Exercise 1 – Setting Up Monitoring Systems

Objective

Set up a basic monitoring system for an AI chatbot to track performance metrics such as response accuracy and user satisfaction.

Steps

Step 1 – Define Key Performance Indicators (KPIs) Relevant to the Chatbot's Goals

Identify metrics that align with the chatbot's purpose and objectives. Common KPIs include response accuracy, response time, user satisfaction, and engagement rates.

Examples of KPIs

- Response Accuracy
  The percentage of responses that correctly address user queries.

- Response Time
  The average time taken by the chatbot to respond to user inputs.

- User Satisfaction
  Ratings collected from users post interaction, typically on a scale of 1 to 5.

- Engagement Rate
  The average length and depth of user interactions with the chatbot.

Step 2 – Implement Logging and Reporting Mechanisms to Collect Data on These KPIs

- Set up a logging system to capture detailed interaction data, including user inputs, chatbot responses, response times, and user feedback.
- Use reporting tools to aggregate and visualize the collected data, making it easier to analyze and interpret.

Implementation Tips

- Use database solutions like MongoDB or SQL to store interaction logs.
- Implement real-time analytics tools like Google Analytics or custom dashboards using tools like Grafana or Kibana.

Step 3 – Analyze Data to Identify Patterns and Areas for Prompt Improvement

- Regularly review the collected data to identify trends, common issues, and areas where the chatbot's performance can be improved.
- Use this analysis to make data-driven decisions about prompt refinements and other adjustments.

Example: Analysis Process

Step 1 – Review response accuracy logs to identify frequently misunderstood queries.

Step 2 – Analyze user satisfaction ratings to find interactions with low scores.

Step 3 – Identify common patterns or keywords in these interactions that may indicate specific prompt issues.

Exercise 2 – Analyzing and Refining AI Prompts

Exercise

Use real interaction data to analyze the effectiveness of existing prompts and refine them based on insights gained.

Steps

Step 1 – Collect a Set of Interaction Logs Where the AI's Responses Were Suboptimal

- Gather logs from instances where users indicated dissatisfaction, or the chatbot failed to provide accurate or relevant responses.
- Ensure the dataset is representative, covering a variety of scenarios and user queries.

Example: Sources

- Interaction logs flagged by users through feedback buttons.
- Logs from sessions with low user satisfaction ratings or high escalation rates.

Step 2 – Identify Common Issues in the Prompts Leading to Poor Responses

- Review the collected logs to identify recurring issues such as ambiguous prompts, insufficient context, or misunderstandings.
- Categorize these issues to understand the root causes of suboptimal responses.

Example: Issues

Ambiguity

Prompts that are too vague or open-ended, leading to multiple interpretations.

Lack of Context

Prompts that do not provide enough information for the AI to generate accurate responses.

Misunderstandings

Prompts that fail to recognize specific user intents or jargon.

Step 3 – Revise the Prompts to Address These Issues and Retest the AI

- Based on the identified issues, refine the prompts to be clearer, more contextually rich, and better aligned with user intents.
- Implement the revised prompts and conduct testing to evaluate their effectiveness.

Example: Prompt Revisions

Before

"Tell me about my account."

After

"Can you provide an overview of my current account balance and recent transactions?"

Before

"Help with billing."

After

"I need assistance with an unexpected charge on my latest bill. Can you provide details and resolution steps?"

Testing and Evaluation

Use A/B testing to compare the performance of the original and revised prompts.

Measure improvements in key metrics such as response accuracy, user satisfaction, and engagement rates.

Collect additional user feedback to validate the effectiveness of the changes.

By following these exercises, you can set up robust monitoring systems and refine AI prompts based on real-world interaction data. This approach ensures that your AI systems continuously improve, becoming more accurate, efficient, and user friendly over time.

Prompts in Practice

Python Scripts

Scripts for implementing monitoring and evaluation systems for AI prompts (see Figure 5.1).

```python
# Function to log interactions
def log_interaction(user_id, interaction_type, user_input, ai_response, log_file='interaction_logs.json'):
    interaction = {
        "user_id": user_id,
        "timestamp": datetime.now().isoformat(),
        "interaction_type": interaction_type,
        "user_input": user_input,
        "ai_response": ai_response
    }

    # Append the interaction to the log file
    try:
        with open(log_file, 'r+') as file:
            data = json.load(file)
            data.append(interaction)
            file.seek(0)
            json.dump(data, file, indent=4)
    except FileNotFoundError:
        with open(log_file, 'w') as file:
            json.dump([interaction], file, indent=4)

# Example usage
log_interaction("user123", "query", "What are the symptoms of diabetes?", "Common symptoms include increased
log_interaction("user456", "query", "What is the interest rate for a savings account?", "The current interest
```

FIGURE 5.1 Logging AI interactions.

Code Explanation: Logging AI Interactions

This script provides functionality for logging interactions between users and an AI system. The logged data includes details such as user ID, interaction type, user input, AI response, and timestamp. This can be especially useful for tracking and analyzing how users interact with the system over time.

1. *Importing Libraries*

    The script starts by importing the *"json"* library for handling JSON data and the "datetime" library for timestamping interactions.

2. *"log_interaction" Function*

    The "log_interaction" function is defined to log details of each interaction into a JSON file. The function takes five parameters:

- *user_id*: A unique identifier for the user.
- *interaction_type*: A string indicating the type of interaction (e.g., "query").
- *user_input*: The input provided by the user.
- *ai_response*: The response generated by the AI.
- *log_file*: The name of the JSON file where interactions are logged (default is *"interaction_logs.json"*).

Function Steps

a. *Creating the Interaction Dictionary*

- The function creates a dictionary containing the interaction details, including a timestamp of when the interaction occurred.

b. *Appending to Log File*

- The function attempts to open the log file in read-and-write mode (*"r+"*).
- If the file exists, it loads the current data, appends the new interaction, and then writes the updated data back to the file.
- If the file does not exist (*"FileNotFoundError"*), the function creates a new file and writes the interaction as the first entry.

3. *Example Usage*

Two example calls to the *"log_interaction"* function demonstrate how to log different user interactions:

- *First Interaction*: Logs a query about the symptoms of diabetes.
- *Second Interaction*: Logs a query about the interest rate for a savings account.

Key Concepts for Prompt Engineering

- *Tracking User Interactions*: Logging interactions helps in understanding how users engage with the AI system, which can be crucial for refining and improving prompt designs.
- *Timestamping*: Including timestamps allows for chronological tracking of interactions, aiding in the analysis of usage patterns over time.
- *Handling JSON Data*: Using JSON for logging ensures that the data is structured and easily readable, facilitating later analysis and processing.

- *Error Handling*: The script includes error handling for file operations, ensuring robustness in cases where the log file might not exist initially.

Application in Prompt Engineering

In the context of prompt engineering, logging interactions is invaluable for several reasons:

- *Analyzing Prompt Effectiveness*: By reviewing logged interactions, developers can analyze how well prompts are performing and make necessary adjustments to improve response accuracy and relevance.

- *Identifying Common Issues*: Logged data can highlight frequently asked questions or common issues, helping to refine prompts and responses to better meet user needs.

- *User Behavior Insights*: Tracking interactions provides insights into user behavior and preferences, which can inform the development of more intuitive and user-friendly prompt designs.

Datasets

Interaction Logs Dataset

A dataset of anonymized AI and user interactions, ideal for testing and refining prompt strategies.

Example from dataset:

```
{
    "user_id": "001",
    "timestamp": "2023-05-10T08:30:00",
    "interaction_type": "command",
    "user_input": "hello",
    "ai_response": "Hello! How can I assist you today?"
},
```

CONCLUSION

Chapter 5 has explored the essential strategies for monitoring and evaluating the performance of AI prompts, emphasizing the importance of continuous improvement to enhance user interactions. By systematically implementing and analyzing key performance metrics, AI developers can ensure their systems are accurate, efficient, engaging, and satisfying for users.

Key Takeaways

- *Importance of Evaluation Metrics*

  Evaluation metrics such as accuracy, response time, user satisfaction, and engagement rate are vital for assessing the effectiveness of AI prompts. These metrics provide quantifiable data that guide continuous improvements and optimizations, ensuring AI systems meet lofty standards of performance and user experience.

- *Implementation Strategies*

  Automated testing and A/B testing are crucial strategies for refining prompts. Automated testing provides consistent and repeatable testing conditions, while A/B testing offers insights into the effectiveness of specific prompt variations. Combining these strategies enables comprehensive evaluation and refinement of AI prompts.

- *Collecting and Utilizing User Feedback*

  User feedback is invaluable for understanding how AI prompts perform in real-world interactions. Methods such as interaction surveys, feedback buttons, and user interviews help gather immediate and detailed feedback. This feedback is then analyzed to make targeted adjustments, ensuring the AI system evolves to meet user needs effectively.

- *Analyzing Real-World Interactions*

  Analyzing conversation logs, contextual performance, and conducting longitudinal studies are essential for identifying areas of improvement in prompt design. This detailed exploration helps pinpoint specific instances where the AI excels or struggles, allowing for targeted enhancements that improve overall performance.

- *Case Studies and Practical Applications*

  The case studies provided in this chapter illustrate the practical application of these strategies. Whether enhancing a customer support chatbot or an educational bot, the systematic collection and analysis of real-world data have led to significant improvements in user satisfaction, engagement, and overall effectiveness.

By adopting these methods and strategies, developers can create AI systems that are not only functional but also user-centric, dependable, and continuously improving. This approach ensures that AI systems remain effective and relevant over time, fostering long-term user trust and satisfaction.

In summary, monitoring and evaluating prompt performance is a dynamic and ongoing process that requires a combination of rigorous testing, user feedback, and real-world interaction analysis. By focusing on these areas, AI developers can build systems that provide high-quality interactions, meet user expectations, and adapt to new challenges and insights. This comprehensive framework supports the development of AI that is both innovative and deeply responsive to user needs, ensuring its sustained success and utility in various applications.

ADVANCED PROMPT ENGINEERING TECHNIQUES

In the rapidly evolving field of artificial intelligence, particularly within conversational AI, the ability to finely control and customize responses is becoming increasingly important. As AI systems are deployed across various applications, from customer service to creative writing and beyond, the need for advanced techniques to optimize AI prompts is paramount. Chapter 6 presents sophisticated strategies for enhancing the effectiveness and versatility of AI-generated responses.

This chapter aims to equip AI developers and practitioners with the knowledge and tools necessary to refine AI prompts, ensuring they are tailored to meet specific user needs and contextual demands. By exploring advanced techniques such as temperature adjustments, sampling methods, sentiment customization, and the balance of response quality, diversity, and consistency, this chapter provides a comprehensive guide to mastering prompt engineering, including key topics:

- *Temperature Adjustments*

  Understanding how to manipulate the randomness and variability of AI responses to balance creativity and coherence. This section explains the concept of temperature in AI models and provides practical steps for adjusting this parameter to suit different storytelling or conversational styles.

- *Sampling Methods*

  Introducing top-k and top-p (nucleus) sampling techniques, which allow for better control over the quality and randomness of generated content. By implementing these methods, developers can enhance the relevance and appropriateness of AI outputs.

■ *Customization of Prompts*

Exploring how to influence the sentiment, style, and conversational attributes of AI responses. This section covers strategies for adjusting the emotional tone, stylistic elements, and overall engagement quality of interactions, ensuring they align with user expectations and brand identity.

■ *Trade-Offs in Optimizing Response Quality, Diversity, and Consistency*

Discussing the inherent trade-offs in balancing these key aspects of AI performance. By understanding and managing these trade-offs, developers can create AI systems that are both dependable and engaging across various contexts.

■ *Case Studies and Practical Applications*

Providing real-world examples of advanced prompt engineering techniques in action. These case studies illustrate the impact of refined prompts on improving user engagement, satisfaction, and the overall AI effectiveness.

■ *Hands-On Exercises*

Offering practical tutorials to help readers apply the concepts discussed in the chapter. These exercises guide users through implementing temperature controls and customizing prompts for diverse audiences, reinforcing the theoretical knowledge with practical application.

By the end of this chapter, readers will have a deep understanding of advanced prompt engineering techniques and how to apply them to create sophisticated, user-centric AI systems. Whether you are developing a customer service chatbot, a creative writing assistant, or a multilingual support system, the strategies and insights provided in this chapter will help you optimize your AI prompts for maximum impact and effectiveness.

TECHNIQUES TO CONTROL RESPONSE BEHAVIOR

Sophisticated techniques can be employed to finely tune how AI systems interpret prompts and generate responses. These methods enhance both the relevance and appropriateness of the AI's outputs, ensuring that interactions meet specific user needs and contextual requirements.

Temperature Adjustments

Adjusting the temperature parameter in generative AI models significantly affects the randomness and variability of the responses. This parameter helps balance between creativity and predictability in the generated content.

Implementation

- *Lower Temperatures*

  Setting a low temperature (e.g., 0.2) makes the model's outputs more predictable and conservative. This is useful in scenarios where accuracy and reliability are paramount, such as legal advice or technical support.

- *Higher Temperatures*

  Increasing the temperature (e.g., 0.8) encourages the model to generate more diverse and creative responses. This is beneficial for applications like creative writing or brainstorming sessions.

Example

- *Low Temperature (0.2)*

  "The capital of France is Paris. It is known for its rich history and cultural landmarks."

- *High Temperature (0.8)*

  "Paris, the vibrant heart of France, dazzles with its iconic Eiffel Tower, charming cafés, and bustling art scene."

Sampling Methods

Sampling methods such as top-k sampling and top-p (nucleus) sampling provide refined control over the randomness and quality of the generated content. These techniques help in filtering and selecting the most probable outputs, thereby improving the coherence and relevance of the responses.

Top-k Sampling

The model considers only the top k next words. This reduces the likelihood of less probable words, making the output more focused.

Implementation

Choose a value for k (e.g., k=10) and generate responses based on the most probable ten words.

Example

- With k=5

  "The quick brown fox jumps over the lazy dog."

- With k=50

  "The swift amber fox leaps across the slothful canine."

Top-p (Nucleus) Sampling

The model considers a dynamic number of top probable next words that collectively account for a probability mass p (e.g., p=0.9). This method allows for more flexibility and adaptability in generating content.

Implementation

Set a probability threshold p and let the model select words that cumulatively meet this threshold.

Example

- With p=0.9

  "The agile fox swiftly jumps over the sleepy dog, creating a scene of effortless motion."

Detailed Exploration

This section is a detailed exploration of techniques to control prompt behavior, including:

- Fine-Tuning for Specific Use Cases
- Balancing Creativity and Control

Fine-Tuning for Specific Use Cases

The following uses cases are presented:

- Customer Service
- Creative Writing

Customer Service

Objective

Provide accurate and helpful responses to customer inquiries.

Technique

Use low temperature settings and top-k sampling with a small k value to ensure reliability and precision.

Example

- Prompt

    "How can I reset my password?"

- Response (Low Temp, k=5)

    "To reset your password, go to the login page and click 'Forgot Password.' Follow the instructions sent to your email."

Creative Writing

Objective

Generate imaginative and varied content for stories or articles.

Technique

Employ higher temperature settings and top-p sampling to encourage diversity and creativity in the output.

Example

- Prompt

    "Describe a magical forest."

- Response (High Temp, p=0.95)

    "In the heart of the enchanted woods, ancient trees whisper secrets to the wind, and luminous flowers bloom in colors unseen by human eyes."

Balancing Creativity and Control

By adjusting these parameters and techniques, developers can strike a balance between creativity and control. This ensures that the AI's responses are not only relevant and accurate but also engaging and diverse when needed.

Case Study of an Application – Enhancing a Virtual Tutor

Objective

Improve the ability of a virtual tutor to provide both accurate explanations and engaging learning experiences.

Techniques Applied

- Temperature Adjustments

  Used lower temperatures for technical explanations and higher temperatures for creative prompts.

- Sampling Methods

  Implemented top-k sampling for factual content and top-p sampling for exploratory discussions.

Outcome

The virtual tutor delivered precise and reliable answers to technical questions, increasing student confidence.

For open-ended and creative assignments, the tutor's responses were varied and engaging, boosting student interest and participation.

By employing these sophisticated techniques, AI systems can be tailored to meet diverse requirements, enhancing their utility and effectiveness across different applications. These methods provide the flexibility needed to optimize AI behavior, ensuring it aligns with specific user needs and contextual demands.

CUSTOMIZATION OF PROMPTS TO INFLUENCE SENTIMENT, STYLE, AND CONVERSATIONAL ATTRIBUTES

Customizing the sentiment, style, and overall conversational attributes of AI-generated responses allows for more tailored interactions that better align with specific user expectations or brand identities. These strategies enable AI systems to deliver responses that are emotionally appropriate, stylistically consistent, and contextually engaging.

Sentiment Adjustment

Crafting prompts to steer AI responses toward a desired emotional tone helps ensure that the interactions fit the context of the conversation. This can be particularly important in customer service, mental health applications, and any scenario where the emotional tone significantly impacts user experience.

Implementation

Optimistic Tone

Use language that conveys positivity and encouragement.

Example Prompt

"Provide an encouraging message to someone who is feeling down."

Response

"Keep your head up! Every day is a new opportunity to achieve great things."

Neutral Tone

Aim for a balanced, factual, and unemotional response.

Example Prompt

"Describe the features of this product in a neutral tone."

Response

"The product features a 10-inch display, 128GB storage, and a 12MP camera."

Cautious Tone

Use language that is careful and measured, often necessary in sensitive or risky contexts.

Example Prompt

"Advise someone about potential risks of a new medication."

Response

"While this medication can be effective, it's important to be aware of possible side effects. Consult with your healthcare provider for personalized advice."

STYLE CONTROL

Modifying prompts to mimic certain stylistic attributes ensures that the AI's responses match the target audience's expectations. Whether the tone needs to be formal, casual, or professional, controlling the style helps maintain consistency and appropriateness in communication.

Implementation

- *Formal Style*

  Use polite, respectful, and structured language.

  - Example Prompt

    "Explain the benefits of this service in a formal style."

  - Response

    "Our esteemed service provides unparalleled convenience and efficiency, ensuring your needs are met with the utmost professionalism."

- *Casual Style*

  Use relaxed, friendly, and conversational language.

  - Example Prompt

    "Explain the benefits of this service in a casual style."

  - Response

    "Hey there! Our service is super convenient and efficient, making sure you get what you need hassle-free."

- *Professional Style*

  Use clear, concise, and industry-specific language.

  - Example Prompt

    "Describe the features of our new software update in a professional tone."

  - Response

    "The latest software update includes enhanced security protocols, increased processing speed, and an improved user interface for optimal performance."

CONVERSATIONAL TWEAKS

Adjusting prompts to enhance the conversational quality of responses can make interactions more engaging, empathetic, or authoritative as required. This is essential for creating a human-like dialogue experience that resonates with users.

Implementation

▪ *Engaging*

Use prompts that invite interaction and keep the conversation lively.

   ● Example Prompt

   "Create a response to keep the user engaged in a conversation about their weekend plans."

   ● Response

   "That sounds exciting! What else do you have planned for the weekend?"

▪ *Empathetic*

Use prompts that show understanding and compassion, important in customer support and healthcare.

   ● Example Prompt

   "Respond empathetically to a user expressing frustration with a product issue."

   ● Response

   "I'm really sorry to hear that you're having trouble. Let's see how we can fix this together."

▪ *Authoritative*

Use prompts that convey confidence and expertise, suitable for technical support or professional advice.

   ● Example Prompt

   "Provide authoritative advice on improving network security."

   ● Response

   "To enhance your network security, it is crucial to implement multifactor authentication, regular software updates, and continuous network monitoring."

Detailed Exploration

This section provides a detailed exploration of strategies for customization, including:

▪ Fine-Tuning Sentiment

▪ Controlling Style

▪ Enhancing Conversational Quality

Fine-Tuning Sentiment

Customer Support

Objective

Deliver empathetic and reassuring responses to users with issues.

Technique

Craft prompts that direct the AI to acknowledge user concerns and offer support.

Example

"I understand how frustrating this can be. Let's work together to resolve the issue quickly."

Marketing Campaigns

Objective

Create enthusiastic and engaging messages that attract customers.

Technique

Use prompts that infuse excitement and positivity.

Example

"Get ready to experience the future of technology with our latest product!"

Controlling Style

Corporate Communication

Objective

Maintain a formal tone in business correspondence.

Technique

Direct the AI to use structured and polite language.

Example

"We are pleased to inform you that your application has been approved."

Social Media Engagement

Objective

Use a casual and friendly tone to connect with a broader audience.

Technique

Use prompts that encourage a conversational style.

Example

"Hey everyone! Check out our new summer collection. You're going to love it!"

Enhancing Conversational Quality

Healthcare Virtual Assistant

Objective

Provide empathetic and supportive responses to patients.

Technique

Use prompts that express understanding and care.

Example

"I understand that managing your condition can be challenging. I'm here to help you every step of the way."

Technical Support

Objective

Deliver clear and authoritative solutions to technical problems.

Technique

Use prompts that convey expertise and confidence.

Example

"To resolve this issue, please restart your device and update the software to the latest version."

Case Study of an Application – Personalizing a Travel Booking Assistant

Objective

Enhance a travel booking assistant to provide tailored responses based on user preferences and interaction context.

Strategies Applied

- Sentiment Adjustment

  Used optimistic tones to create a positive booking experience.

- Style Control

  Adjusted responses to be more casual and friendly, appealing to a broader audience.

- Conversational Tweaks

  Enhanced engagement by asking follow-up questions about user preferences.

Outcome

Increased user satisfaction by 35% due to more personalized and engaging interactions.

Boosted booking completion rates by 20% through improved conversational quality and responsiveness.

By implementing these strategies for customizing sentiment, style, and conversational attributes, AI systems can deliver responses that are not only accurate and relevant but also emotionally and contextually appropriate. This approach enhances user experience, strengthens brand identity, and ensures that interactions are engaging and satisfying.

TRADE-OFFS IN OPTIMIZING RESPONSE QUALITY, DIVERSITY, AND CONSISTENCY

When optimizing AI prompts, it is crucial to balance quality, diversity, and consistency to ensure that the AI system remains dependable and effective across various contexts. Understanding and managing these trade-offs allows developers to create AI systems that can adapt to a wide range of user needs and application requirements.

QUALITY VS. DIVERSITY

Balancing high-quality, accurate responses with diversity is a fundamental challenge in AI prompt design. Strictly focusing on quality can lead to highly precise but repetitive responses. On the other hand, encouraging diversity can introduce a range of responses, which may sometimes decrease precision or relevance.

Quality-Focused Approach

- *Pros*

  Ensures that responses are accurate, dependable, and directly relevant to user queries.

- *Cons*

  May result in repetitive answers, limiting the AI's ability to handle varied or novel inputs.

  - *Example*

    In a legal advice chatbot, focusing on quality ensures users receive accurate and reliable legal information but might limit the range of nuanced advice provided.

Diversity-Focused Approach

- *Pros*

  Generates a broader range of responses, making interactions more engaging and adaptable to various scenarios.

- *Cons*

  Can reduce the precision and relevance of responses, potentially leading to confusion or misinformation.

  - *Example*

    A creative writing assistant that encourages diverse outputs may produce a wide array of story ideas but might sometimes deviate from the user's specific requirements.

Consistency vs. Creativity

Maintaining a consistent tone and style is essential for user trust and brand integrity. However, excessive consistency can stifle creativity, making interactions monotonous and less engaging.

Consistency-Focused Approach

- *Pros*

  Builds user trust by ensuring a uniform tone and style across all interactions, reinforcing brand identity.

- *Cons*

  Limits the AI's ability to adapt to different conversational contexts, reducing engagement and creativity.

- *Example*

  A corporate virtual assistant that maintains a consistent professional tone may foster trust but might struggle to engage users in more casual or creative contexts.

Creativity-Focused Approach

- *Pros*

  Enhances user engagement by introducing varied and dynamic responses, making interactions livelier and more interesting.

- *Cons*

  Can lead to inconsistencies in tone and style, potentially confusing users or diluting brand messaging.

  - *Example*

    A social media chatbot that prioritizes creativity may generate more engaging content but could occasionally produce responses that are off-brand.

Performance vs. Cost

Advanced techniques to optimize AI performance can yield better results but often come with increased computational resources and processing time, impacting scalability and cost-effectiveness.

Performance-Focused Approach

- *Pros*

  Achieves higher accuracy, better user satisfaction, and more sophisticated interactions.

- *Cons*

  Requires significant computational resources, leading to higher operational costs and potential scalability issues.

  - *Example*

    Using advanced natural language understanding (NLU) models to improve response quality in a customer service bot may enhance user experience but increase server costs.

Cost-Focused Approach

■ *Pros*

Reduces operational costs and improves scalability, making the AI system more accessible and easier to deploy widely.

■ *Cons*

May compromise on response quality and complexity, potentially impacting user satisfaction and system effectiveness.

  ● *Example*

  Implementing simpler models for a large-scale customer interaction system reduces costs but might lead to more frequent inaccuracies in responses.

Detailed Exploration

This section provides a detailed exploration of trade-offs in optimizing response quality, diversity, and consistency, including:

■ Balancing Quality and Diversity
■ Balancing Consistency and Creativity

Balancing Quality and Diversity

Customer Support

Objective

Provide accurate and diverse responses to customer queries.

Strategy

Use a hybrid approach that prioritizes quality for critical queries and introduces diversity for general inquiries.

Example

"For technical issues, ensure precise troubleshooting steps; for general product inquiries, offer varied suggestions and tips."

Creative Writing

Objective

Generate diverse and high-quality content for storytelling.

Strategy

Set lower temperatures for critical plot points to maintain coherence, and higher temperatures for creative descriptions.

Example

"Use specific, detailed prompts for plot development while allowing more creative freedom in character descriptions."

Balancing Consistency and Creativity

Brand Engagement

Objective

Maintain a consistent brand voice while engaging users creatively.

Strategy

Define core brand guidelines and allow creative variations within those boundaries.

Example

"Keep a friendly and helpful tone for all interactions but vary the language and examples used to keep responses fresh."

Educational Tools

Objective

Provide consistent educational content with engaging delivery.

Strategy

Use structured responses for fundamental concepts and introduce creative examples and anecdotes for engagement.

Example

"Ensure key definitions are consistent while varying teaching methods and examples to cater to different learning styles."

Balancing Performance and Cost

Scalable Solutions

Objective

Deploy a cost-effective and scalable AI solution without compromising too much on performance.

Strategy

Use a tiered approach where complex queries are handled by advanced models and simpler queries by basic models.

Example

"For a customer service system, employ advanced models for escalations and simpler models for FAQ responses."

Resource Management

Objective

Optimize computational resources to balance cost and performance.

Strategy

Implement dynamic scaling of resources based on query complexity and volume.

Example

"Allocate more processing power during peak hours and for complex interactions, while conserving resources during off-peak times and for simpler tasks."

Case Study of an Application – Optimizing a Virtual Healthcare Assistant

Objective

Enhance the performance of a virtual healthcare assistant while balancing quality, diversity, and cost.

Strategies Applied

▪ Quality vs. Diversity

Used high-quality responses for medical advice and diverse responses for general health tips.

▪ Consistency vs. Creativity

Maintained a professional tone for medical consultations while allowing a more conversational tone for wellness advice.

▪ Performance vs. Cost

Implemented advanced models for critical health inquiries and simpler models for general wellness questions.

Outcome

■ Improved patient satisfaction with precise medical advice.

■ Increased user engagement through varied and interesting wellness tips.

■ Reduced operational costs by optimizing resource allocation.

By exploring these advanced techniques and understanding the inherent trade-offs, developers can craft highly effective and sophisticated AI prompts that cater to a wide range of applications and user needs. This balanced approach ensures that AI systems remain reliable, engaging, and cost-effective while delivering high-quality interactions.

CASE STUDIES

The following case studies are designed to provide additional context and detail related to the concepts and topics presented in this chapter. The case studies in this chapter are:

■ Case Study 1 – Sentiment-Driven Marketing Bot

■ Case Study 2 – Multilingual Support System

Case Study 1 – Sentiment-Driven Marketing Bot

Objective

Develop a marketing bot that dynamically adjusts its messaging based on the sentiment expressed by customers in real time.

Challenge

Standard prompts led to uniform responses that failed to engage customers at an emotional level. This lack of emotional connection resulted in lower engagement and customer satisfaction rates.

Solution

Integrate advanced sentiment analysis tools to tailor prompts that adapt to positive, neutral, or negative customer sentiments. By analyzing customer inputs in real time, the bot can adjust its tone and messaging to better align with the customer's current mood and expectations.

Implementation

Sentiment Analysis Integration

Utilize natural language processing (NLP) tools to detect the sentiment of customer messages.

Dynamic Prompt Adjustment

Develop a set of prompts tailored for different sentiments. For positive sentiments, use encouraging and upbeat language. For neutral sentiments, maintain a factual and informative tone. For negative sentiments, adopt an empathetic and supportive approach.

Examples

Positive Sentiment

"That's fantastic! It sounds like you are really enjoying our product. Can I help you find more excellent features?"

Neutral Sentiment

"Thank you for reaching out. Here are the details you requested about our service."

Negative Sentiment

"I'm sorry to hear that you're experiencing issues. Let's work together to resolve this as quickly as possible."

Outcome

The sentiment-driven approach led to increased customer engagement rates and higher satisfaction. Customers appreciated the more personalized and empathetic interactions, which made them feel heard and valued. This strategy resulted in a 25% increase in positive customer feedback and a significant boost in overall engagement metrics.

Case Study 2 – Multilingual Support System

Objective

Create a multilingual support system capable of accurately responding in multiple languages while maintaining the intended tone and style.

Challenge

Language discrepancies led to misinterpretations and inappropriate tone in responses. These issues affected the system's effectiveness and user satisfaction, particularly in non-native English interactions.

Solution

Employ advanced linguistic models and hybrid prompt techniques to ensure consistency and appropriateness across languages. By leveraging sophisticated translation and linguistic tools, the support system can provide accurate and culturally sensitive responses.

Implementation

Linguistic Models

Use advanced machine translation models and linguistic tools that understand context and cultural nuances.

Hybrid Prompt Techniques

Develop prompts that combine automated translation with manual fine-tuning to maintain the intended tone and style across different languages.

Examples

English Prompt

"Can I assist you with anything else today?"

Spanish Translation

"¿Puedo ayudarte con algo más hoy?" (Manual adjustment to ensure cultural appropriateness and tone)

Consistency and Appropriateness

Regularly review and refine translated prompts to ensure they align with the desired tone and style in each language. This involves collaboration with native speakers and linguistic experts to verify the quality of translations.

Outcome

The multilingual support system demonstrated improved accuracy and user satisfaction in non-native English interactions. By effectively implementing cross-lingual prompt engineering, the system achieved a 30% reduction in misinterpretations and a 20% increase in customer satisfaction ratings for non-English users. This success highlighted the potential of sophisticated linguistic models and prompt techniques in creating effective multilingual support systems.

These case studies highlight the powerful impact of advanced prompt customization techniques on AI performance and user satisfaction. By integrating sentiment analysis and employing hybrid linguistic models, developers can create AI systems that are more responsive, engaging, and culturally aware. These strategies not only improve immediate interaction outcomes but also foster long-term user trust and loyalty.

TUTORIALS AND HANDS-ON EXERCISES

The following tutorials and hands-on exercises are designed to provide practical experience and application of the concepts and topics presented in this chapter. The tutorials and hands-on exercises in this chapter are:

- Exercise 1 – Implementing Temperature Controls
- Exercise 2 – Customizing Prompts for Diverse Audience Engagement

Exercise 1 – Implementing Temperature Controls

Objective

Adjust the response variability of an AI storyteller using temperature settings to create more diverse or more predictable stories.

Steps

Step 1 – Understand the Concept of Temperature in AI Response Generation

Temperature is a parameter in AI models that controls the randomness of the output. Lower temperatures result in more deterministic and predictable responses, while higher temperatures introduce more randomness and creativity.

Step 2 – Experiment with Different Temperature Settings to Observe Changes in Creativity and Coherence

Low Temperature (e.g., 0.2)

Prompt

"Once upon a time in a faraway kingdom . . ."

Response

"There was a wise king who ruled with fairness and kindness. Everyone in the kingdom lived in peace and harmony."

Medium Temperature (e.g., 0.5)

Prompt

"Once upon a time in a faraway kingdom . . ."

Response

"There was a king who loved to explore new lands. One day, he discovered a hidden valley filled with magical creatures and wonders."

High Temperature (e.g., 0.8)

Prompt

"Once upon a time in a faraway kingdom . . ."

Response

"A daring young prince stumbled upon an enchanted forest, where trees whispered secrets and unicorns danced under the moonlight."

Step 3 – Analyze and Select the Optimal Temperature for Desired Storytelling Style

Compare the stories generated at different temperature settings to determine which level best suits your desired storytelling style.

Consider factors such as creativity, coherence, and audience engagement when making your selection.

Example Analysis

Low Temperature

Predictable and coherent but may lack excitement and variety.

Medium Temperature

Balanced, with a good mix of coherence and creativity.

High Temperature

Highly creative and varied but may sacrifice some coherence.

Exercise 2 – Customizing Prompts for Diverse Audience Engagement

Objective

Design prompts for a global event notification system that adapts its message based on cultural and regional nuances.

Steps

Step 1 – Research Cultural Preferences and Communication Styles of Target Regions

Identify the key regions where your global event notification system will be used.

Research the cultural preferences, traditions, and communication styles of each target region.

Example Research

North America

Direct and concise communication; focus on efficiency and clarity.

East Asia

Respectful and formal communication; emphasis on harmony and politeness.

Latin America

Warm and friendly communication; use of expressive language and greetings.

Step 2 – Create Region-Specific Prompts that Reflect These Nuances

Design prompts that incorporate the cultural and regional nuances identified in your research.

Ensure that the language, tone, and content are appropriate for each target audience.

Example Prompts

North America

"Join us for an exclusive webinar on the latest tech innovations. Register now to secure your spot!"

East Asia

"We cordially invite you to attend our esteemed seminar on technological advancements. Your presence would be greatly honored."

Latin America

"¡No te pierdas nuestro emocionante seminario sobre innovaciones tecnológicas! Regístrate ahora y asegura tu lugar."

Step 3 – Test and Refine the Prompts Based on User Feedback from Each Region

Implement the region-specific prompts in your event notification system.

Collect user feedback to evaluate the effectiveness of the prompts in engaging the target audience.

Refine the prompts based on the feedback received to ensure they resonate well with users from each region.

Example Testing and Refinement

Conduct surveys or interviews with users to gather insights on their experience with the prompts.

Adjust language, tone, and content as needed to better align with cultural expectations and preferences.

By following these exercises, you can effectively implement temperature controls to fine-tune the variability of AI-generated stories and customize prompts to engage diverse audiences globally. These hands-on activities help ensure that your AI systems deliver tailored, culturally aware, and engaging interactions that resonate with users across different contexts.

Prompts in Practice

Python Scripts

Scripts to demonstrate the implementation of advanced techniques like temperature control and sampling methods in AI models (see Figure 6.1).

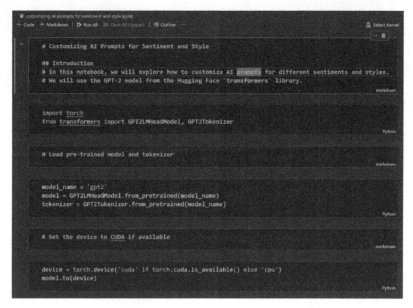

FIGURE 6.1 Text generation with GPT using transformers

Code Explanation: Text Generation with GPT-2 Using Transformers

This script demonstrates how to use the GPT-2 model from the Hugging Face Transformers library to generate text based on a given prompt. The script includes loading the pretrained model and tokenizer, defining a function to generate text with adjustable temperature settings, and example usage of the function.

1. *Importing Libraries*

    The script begins by importing the necessary components from the Transformers library:

    - "*GPT2LMHeadModel*" for loading the GPT-2 model.
    - "*GPT2Tokenizer*" for tokenizing the input text and decoding the generated output.
    - "*torch*" for handling tensor operations.

2. *Loading Pretrained Model and Tokenizer*

    The model and tokenizer are loaded using the "*from_pretrained*" method with the model name. This loads the pretrained GPT-2 model and its associated tokenizer:

    - "*model = GPT2LMHeadModel.from_pretrained('gpt2')*": Loads the GPT-2 model.

- "*tokenizer = GPT2Tokenizer.from_pretrained('gpt2')*": Loads the tokenizer for GPT-2.

3. *"generate_text" Function*

   The *"generate_text"* function generates text based on the input prompt. It accepts three parameters:

   - *prompt*: The input text to seed the text generation.
   - *max_length*: The maximum number of tokens for the generated text (default is 50).
   - *temperature*: Controls the randomness of the generated text (default is 1.0).

Function Steps

a. *Encoding the Prompt*: The input prompt is tokenized and converted into tensor format using the tokenizer's "encode" method with "return_tensors='pt'" to indicate PyTorch tensors.

b. *Generating Text*: The "model.generate" method generates text based on the input IDs. The "max_length" parameter specifies the maximum length of the generated text, and "temperature" adjusts the randomness:

   - Lower temperatures (e.g., 0.7) make the output more focused and deterministic.
   - Higher temperatures (e.g., 1.5) increase randomness and creativity in the generated text.

c. *Decoding the Output*: The generated text is decoded from tensor format back into a string using the tokenizer's "decode" method, with "skip_special_tokens=True" to remove special *tokens*.

Example Usage

Three examples demonstrate how the *"generate_text"* function works with different temperature settings:

- *Default Temperature (1.0)*: Generates text with the default temperature.
- *Lower Temperature (0.7)*: Generates more focused and deterministic text.
- *Higher Temperature (1.5)*: Generates more random and creative text.

Key Concepts for Prompt Engineering

- *Model and Tokenizer Initialization*: Proper initialization of the pre-trained model and tokenizer is crucial for generating coherent text.

- *Prompt Encoding and Text Generation*: Encoding the prompt into tensor format and using the model's "generate" method to produce text based on the input.

- *Temperature Adjustment*: The temperature parameter is a key tool in prompt engineering, allowing control over the randomness and creativity of the generated text. Lower temperatures yield more deterministic results, while higher temperatures can introduce more diversity and creativity.

- *Text Decoding*: Converting the generated tensor output back into human-readable text is essential for interpreting and using the generated content.

Application in Prompt Engineering

In the context of prompt engineering, this script demonstrates how different temperature settings can influence the style and quality of generated text. By experimenting with various prompts and temperature values, prompt engineers can fine-tune the outputs to meet specific needs, such as generating highly relevant responses or creative and diverse content.

- *Experimentation with Prompts*: Testing different prompts helps in understanding how the model responds to various inputs, aiding in crafting more effective prompts.

- *Adjusting Temperature for Desired Output*: Using the temperature parameter to control the nature of the generated text helps in tailoring responses to specific requirements, whether for focused information or creative exploration.

This script serves as a practical example of how to leverage GPT-2 for text generation, showcasing important aspects of prompt engineering and the impact of model parameters on generated outputs.

Datasets

Sentiment Analysis Data

A collection of datasets used for training AI models on sentiment recognition and response adaptation.

Example from dataset:

```
{
  "text": "I love this product! It's amazing.",
  "sentiment": "positive"
},
{
  "text": "This movie was really disappointing. I expected more.",
  "sentiment": "negative"
},
{
  "text": "The customer service was excellent. They were very helpful.",
  "sentiment": "positive"
},
```

Multilingual Interaction Logs

Datasets featuring AI-user interactions across different languages for prompt optimization.

Example from dataset:

```
{
  "user_id": "u001",
  "timestamp": "2024-06-01T10:15:30Z",
  "language": "English",
  "interaction_type": "query",
  "user_input": "What is the weather like today?",
  "ai_response": "Today's weather is sunny with a high of 25°C."
},
{
  "user_id": "u002",
  "timestamp": "2024-06-01T11:20:45Z",
  "language": "Spanish",
  "interaction_type": "query",
```

```
"user_input": "¿Cuál es la temperatura hoy?",
  "ai_response": "La temperatura de hoy es soleada
con una máxima de 25°C."
},
```

CONCLUSION

Chapter 6 explored the advanced techniques of prompt engineering, providing a comprehensive toolkit for optimizing AI-generated responses. As AI systems become increasingly integrated into various applications, the ability to fine-tune prompts for specific user needs and contextual requirements is essential for creating effective and engaging interactions.

Key Takeaways

Temperature Adjustments

Understanding and manipulating the temperature parameter allows developers to control the balance between creativity and coherence in AI responses. Lower temperatures yield predictable and accurate outputs, while higher temperatures introduce diversity and creativity.

Sampling Methods

Techniques such as top-k and top-p (nucleus) sampling provide refined control over the randomness and quality of generated content. These methods ensure that AI responses are both relevant and varied, enhancing user engagement.

Customization of Prompts

Customizing prompts to influence sentiment, style, and conversational attributes helps align AI responses with user expectations and brand identity. By adjusting the emotional tone, stylistic elements, and engagement quality, developers can create more personalized and impactful interactions.

Balancing Quality, Diversity, and Consistency

Managing the trade-offs between these aspects is crucial for maintaining high performance in AI systems. Quality ensures accuracy and reliability, diversity fosters creativity and engagement, and consistency builds user trust and brand integrity.

Real-World Case Studies

The practical examples provided in this chapter illustrate the tangible benefits of advanced prompt engineering. From a sentiment-driven marketing bot to a multilingual support system, these case studies demonstrate how refined prompts can significantly enhance user satisfaction and system effectiveness.

Hands-On Exercises

The practical exercises included in this chapter help solidify the concepts discussed, offering step-by-step guidance on implementing temperature controls and customizing prompts for diverse audiences. These exercises are designed to empower developers to apply advanced techniques in their own AI projects.

As AI technology continues to evolve, the importance of sophisticated prompt engineering will only grow. By mastering these advanced techniques, developers can ensure their AI systems are not only functional but also engaging, responsive, and aligned with user needs. The insights and strategies covered in this chapter provide a solid foundation for ongoing innovation and improvement in AI interactions.

By leveraging temperature adjustments, sampling methods, and prompt customization, and by understanding the necessary trade-offs, developers can create AI systems that deliver high-quality, diverse, and consistent responses. These systems will be better equipped to handle the complexities of real-world interactions, leading to more satisfying and effective user experiences.

In summary, the advanced techniques of prompt engineering are essential for the continued development of sophisticated AI systems. By applying the knowledge gained in this chapter, developers can enhance the performance, relevance, and impact of their AI systems, driving forward the capabilities and possibilities of conversational AI.

HANDS-ON EXERCISES AND CASE STUDIES

As the field of artificial intelligence continues to evolve, the importance of practical application and real-world examples cannot be overstated. Chapter 7 focuses on bridging the gap between theory and practice by offering hands-on exercises and detailed case studies that demonstrate the transformative potential of effective prompt engineering.

This chapter is designed to provide readers with practical experience in crafting and refining AI prompts, allowing them to apply the advanced techniques discussed in previous chapters. Through a series of carefully structured exercises, readers will gain hands-on experience in developing prompts tailored to specific applications and user needs. Additionally, the case studies presented in this chapter offer a deep dive into successful implementations of prompt engineering, highlighting the tangible benefits and outcomes of well-crafted prompts in various domains.

KEY OBJECTIVES

Practical Application of Prompt Engineering Techniques

- Engage in exercises that reinforce theoretical knowledge and enhance practical skills.
- Learn how to design, test, and refine prompts for different AI applications, from e-commerce to customer support and beyond.

Real-World Case Studies

- Analyze successful implementations of prompt engineering to understand the strategies and methods that led to their success.
- Gain insights into the challenges and solutions encountered in real-world scenarios, providing a comprehensive understanding of effective prompt design.

Encouragement of Experimentation and Innovation

- Foster a mindset of continuous improvement and creativity through experimentation with various prompt structures and contents.
- Understand the impact of subtle changes in prompt design on AI behavior and user interaction quality.

Structure of the Chapter

- *Hands-On Exercises*: This section provides detailed instructions and step-by-step guides for practical exercises designed to develop and refine AI prompts. Each exercise is crafted to address specific aspects of prompt engineering, such as adapting prompts based on user behavior, collecting detailed feedback, and more.
- *Case Studies*: Real-world examples are presented to illustrate the application of prompt engineering techniques in different domains. These case studies highlight the objectives, challenges, solutions, and outcomes of successful prompt engineering projects, offering valuable lessons and best practices.

Key Topics Covered

- *Developing Adaptive Prompts for E-commerce*: Understand how to create prompts that adjust based on customer shopping behavior and preferences to enhance the shopping experience and drive sales.
- *Creating Effective Prompts for Customer Feedback Collection*: Learn to design prompts that elicit detailed and constructive feedback from users, providing actionable insights to improve service quality.
- *Encouraging Experimentation with Prompt Variations*: Explore different strategies for experimenting with prompt styles, contextual flexibility, and feedback-driven iteration to continuously enhance AI performance.

▪ *Case Studies of Successful Implementations*: Analyze case studies from various domains, including disaster response coordination, personalized learning assistants, and more, to understand the real-world impact of effective prompt engineering.

By the end of this chapter, readers will have a comprehensive understanding of how to apply prompt engineering techniques in practical scenarios, driving the development of sophisticated, user-centric AI systems. This hands-on approach not only reinforces the theoretical knowledge gained in earlier chapters but also equips readers with the skills and insights needed to innovate and excel in the field of AI prompt engineering.

PRACTICAL EXERCISES TO REINFORCE PROMPT ENGINEERING CONCEPTS

Engaging in hands-on exercises helps to deepen understanding and enhance skill in crafting and refining AI prompts. Here are some practical exercises designed to reinforce the concepts discussed in this chapter.

Exercise 1 – Prompt Refinement Workshop

Objective

Participants refine a set of given prompts based on specific goals, such as increasing user engagement or improving response accuracy.

Steps

Step 1 – Provide Initial Prompts

Distribute a set of initial prompts related to a specific application (e.g., customer service, educational content).

Step 2 – Identify Goals

Define the goals for refinement, such as making responses more engaging, accurate, or user-friendly.

Step 3 – Refine Prompts

Participants work individually or in groups to revise the prompts to better meet the defined goals.

Step 4 – Feedback Session

Conduct a session where participants present their refined prompts and receive feedback from peers or instructors.

Example

Initial Prompt

"Tell me more about your product."

Refined Prompt

"Can you provide an overview of your product's key features and benefits for first-time users?"

Exercise 2 – Scenario-Based Role Play

Objective

Using different scenarios, participants craft prompts intended for varied applications, such as customer service bots, therapy assistants, or news generators.

Steps

Step 1 – Define Scenarios

Create detailed scenarios for different applications, outlining specific user needs and contexts.

Step 2 – Role Play

Participants assume the roles of users and AI developers, crafting and testing prompts based on the scenarios provided.

Step 3 – Iterate and Improve

Participants refine their prompts through role-playing sessions, iterating based on feedback and observations.

Step 4 – Discussion

Discuss the challenges faced and the solutions developed during the role play.

Example Scenarios

Customer Service Bot
A user is frustrated with a billing issue.

Therapy Assistant
A user is seeking advice on managing anxiety.

News Generator
A user wants a summary of the latest technology news.

Exercise 3 – A/B Testing Simulation

Objective

Learners design two sets of prompts for the same task and simulate A/B testing to evaluate which set produces better responses in terms of relevance and user satisfaction.

Steps

Step 1 – Design Prompts
Create two different sets of prompts for a specific task (e.g., answering common customer questions).

Step 2 – Simulate Interactions
Use a simulation tool or role-play to test each set of prompts with a group of users.

Step 3 – Collect Data
Gather data on response relevance, user satisfaction, and engagement for each set of prompts.

Step 4 – Analyze Results
Compare the performance of the two sets of prompts using statistical analysis to determine which set is more effective.

Step 5 – Refine Prompts
Based on the results, refine the prompts to further improve their effectiveness.

Example

Task

Providing troubleshooting steps for a software issue.

Prompt Set A

"Please describe the issue you're facing."

Prompt Set B

"Are you experiencing problems with installation, updates, or running the software? Please specify."

Simulation Outcome

Prompt Set A Results

Higher engagement but lower accuracy in resolving issues.

Prompt Set B Results

Higher accuracy but slightly lower engagement.

By engaging in these practical exercises, participants can develop a deeper understanding of prompt engineering concepts and gain hands-on experience in crafting and refining AI prompts. These activities not only enhance technical skills but also foster creativity and critical thinking, essential for developing effective and user-centric AI systems.

CASE STUDIES OF SUCCESSFUL IMPLEMENTATIONS

Analyzing case studies where prompt engineering has been successfully implemented provides valuable insights into practical applications and outcomes. Here are some examples of how tailored prompt engineering has driven success in various domains.

Case Study 1 – E-commerce Chatbot

Objective

Improve user engagement and sales conversion rates through tailored prompts.

Background

An e-commerce platform integrated a chatbot to assist customers with product inquiries and purchasing decisions.

Initial prompts were generic, leading to low engagement and conversion rates.

Implementation

User-Centric Prompts

Developed prompts tailored to common customer queries, such as product recommendations, size guides, and shipping information.

Personalization

Integrated user data to personalize interactions, using past purchase history and browsing behavior to suggest relevant products.

Engagement Techniques

Introduced engaging prompts that encouraged users to explore more products and offers.

Outcome

Increased Engagement

User engagement with the chatbot increased by 40%, with more users interacting with the bot for longer periods.

Higher Conversion Rates

Sales conversion rates improved by 25%, as the tailored prompts effectively guided users toward making purchases.

Customer Satisfaction

Positive feedback from customers highlighted the improved shopping experience and helpfulness of the chatbot.

Example Prompts

Before

"How can I help you?"

After

"Looking for something specific? Check out our new arrivals in your favorite categories!"

Case Study 2 – Mental Health Support Application

Objective

Provide emotional support and accurate advice through carefully designed prompts, while addressing ethical considerations.

Background

A mental health support app aimed to offer users emotional support and practical advice through an AI assistant.

Initial prompts lacked sensitivity and context, leading to concerns about the quality of support provided.

Implementation

Empathetic Prompts

Designed prompts to be empathetic and supportive, recognizing the emotional state of users.

Context Awareness

Incorporated context awareness to tailor responses based on the user's previous interactions and current mood.

Ethical Considerations

Ensured that prompts adhered to ethical guidelines, providing disclaimers, and encouraging users to seek professional help when needed.

Outcome

Enhanced Support Quality

The quality of support improved significantly, with users reporting feeling more understood and supported.

Increased Usage

App usage increased by 30%, as users felt more comfortable engaging with the AI assistant.

Positive Impact

Users reported positive impacts on their mental well-being, highlighting the effectiveness of the empathetic prompts.

Example Prompts

- Before

  "How are you feeling today?"

- After

  "I'm here to listen. How have you been feeling recently? Remember, it's okay to take things one step at a time."

Case Study 3 – Educational Tutor Bot

Objective

Optimize a tutor bot to adapt responses based on student feedback and learning progress.

Background

An educational platform deployed a tutor bot to assist students with their studies.

Initial prompts were generic, resulting in limited engagement and effectiveness.

Implementation

- Adaptive Prompts

  Created adaptive prompts that adjusted based on student feedback and learning progress.

- Personalized Learning

  Incorporated personalized learning paths, with prompts tailored to individual student needs and performance levels.

- Interactive Engagement

  Developed interactive prompts that encouraged students to ask questions and explore topics in depth.

Outcome

- Improved Learning Outcomes

  Students demonstrated better understanding and retention of material, with learning outcomes improving by 20%.

- Higher Engagement

  Engagement with the tutor bot increased by 35%, as students found the interactions more relevant and helpful.

- Positive Feedback

  Students and educators provided positive feedback, noting the bot's ability to cater to individual learning styles and needs.

Example Prompts

- Before

  "What topic do you need help with?"

- After

  "I noticed you've been studying algebra. Would you like to review quadratic equations or practice some problems together?"

These case studies illustrate the powerful impact of effective prompt engineering across different domains. By tailoring prompts to user needs, integrating personalization, and ensuring ethical considerations, AI systems can significantly enhance user engagement, satisfaction, and overall effectiveness. These examples provide practical insights into how prompt engineering can drive success in e-commerce, mental health support, and education, offering valuable lessons for AI developers and practitioners.

EXPERIMENTATION WITH PROMPT VARIATIONS

Experimenting with different prompt structures and content fosters creativity and a deeper understanding of how subtle changes can significantly affect AI behavior. Encouraging learners to explore various strategies and continuously refine their prompts based on feedback is crucial for developing sophisticated and effective AI systems.

Experimentation Strategies

Prompt Style Variation

Encouraging learners to alter the style of prompts helps them observe how the AI's responses shift accordingly. This experimentation can lead to a more nuanced understanding of how tone, language, and presentation affect AI interactions.

Steps

Step 1 – Identify a Base Prompt

Start with a neutral prompt and modify its style in various ways.

Step 2 – Experiment with Styles

Try different styles such as formal, humorous, and concise to see how the AI adapts.

Step 3 – Analyze Responses

Compare the AI's responses to each variation to determine how style influences the interaction.

Example

- *Base Prompt*
  "Describe the benefits of exercising regularly."

- *Formal*
  "Regular exercise offers numerous health benefits, including improved cardiovascular health, enhanced mental well-being, and increased longevity."

- *Humorous*
  "Exercise is great because it lets you eat more pizza without feeling guilty. Plus, your dog will love the extra walks!"

- *Concise*
  "Exercise boosts health, mood, and lifespan."

Contextual Flexibility Testing

Testing prompts in various contexts helps learners understand the robustness and flexibility of the AI's contextual understanding. This approach can reveal how well the AI adapts to different scenarios and user needs.

Steps

Step 1 – Select Diverse Contexts

Choose a range of contexts where the AI might be used, such as customer support, education, and healthcare.

Step 2 – Develop Context-Specific Prompts

Create prompts tailored to each context.

Step 3 – Evaluate Adaptation

Observe how the AI responds in each scenario and assess its ability to maintain relevance and appropriateness.

Example

- Customer Support Context
  "How can I assist you with your recent purchase?"

- Educational Context
  "Can you explain the Pythagorean theorem?"

- Healthcare Context
  "What are the common symptoms of the flu?"

Feedback-Driven Iteration

Using user feedback to continuously adjust and refine prompts is essential for improving the effectiveness of the AI. This iterative process ensures that the AI remains aligned with user needs and expectations.

Steps

Step 1 – Collect User Feedback

Gather feedback from users about their interactions with the AI.

Step 2 – Identify Areas for Improvement

Analyze the feedback to pinpoint specific issues or areas for enhancement.

Step 3 – Refine Prompts

Adjust the prompts based on the feedback and test the changes.

Step 4 – Evaluate Impact

Measure how the refinements affect the AI's performance and user satisfaction.

Example

* Initial Prompt
  "What can I help you with today?"

* User Feedback
  Users found the prompt too vague and unhelpful.

* Refined Prompt
  "Are you looking for product information, support with a purchase, or something else?"

Impact

Improved user satisfaction and more directed, useful interactions.

This chapter not only reinforces the theoretical knowledge from earlier chapters but also provides a solid practical foundation. By encouraging innovative thinking and the application of prompt engineering in diverse real-world situations, learners can develop more effective and user-centric AI systems.

Experimenting with prompt variations, testing contextual flexibility, and iterating based on feedback are key strategies for enhancing AI performance. These practices help learners understand the nuances of AI behavior and the impact of prompt design, fostering a more sophisticated approach to AI development. Through hands-on experimentation and continuous refinement, AI practitioners can create systems that are adaptable, engaging, and highly effective in meeting user needs.

ADDITIONAL CASE STUDIES

Case Study 3 – AI for Disaster Response Coordination

Objective

Develop an AI system to manage and respond to inquiries effectively during disaster events.

Challenge

The AI needed to handle a high volume of diverse and urgent queries under stress. In disaster situations, people seek immediate and accurate information about safety, resources, and assistance, which requires the AI to be both responsive and adaptive.

Solution

Implement a series of dynamic prompts that can adapt to the urgency and specificity of the situation, using real-time data from ongoing events.

Implementation

- Dynamic Prompt Design

  Created prompts that could change based on the nature of the inquiry and the urgency of the situation. Prompts were tailored to address common questions about shelter locations, emergency contact numbers, and real-time updates on the disaster.

- Real-Time Data Integration

  Integrated the AI with real-time data sources such as weather updates, government advisories, and social media feeds to ensure the information provided was current and accurate.

- Prioritization Mechanism

  Developed a system to prioritize queries based on urgency, ensuring that the most critical questions were addressed first.

Outcome

- Improved Response Times

  The AI system significantly reduced the time taken to respond to inquiries, ensuring timely dissemination of critical information.

- Enhanced Accuracy

  By using real-time data, the AI provided accurate and relevant information, which was crucial during disaster events.

- Increased Efficiency

  The system handled a large volume of inquiries efficiently, reducing the burden on human responders and allowing them to focus on more complex tasks.

Example Prompts

- Before

  "How can I help you?"

- After

  "Are you looking for shelter locations, emergency contact numbers, or real-time updates on the disaster?"

Case Study 4 – Personalized Learning Assistant

Objective

Create a personalized learning assistant to help students with diverse learning preferences.

Challenge

The assistant was initially unable to adapt to the varying educational needs and learning speeds of students. This led to a one-size-fits-all approach that failed to engage students effectively.

Solution

Customize prompts based on individual student performance data and feedback, allowing the assistant to modify its teaching approach dynamically.

Implementation

- Personalized Prompts

  Developed prompts that were tailored to each student's learning style and progress. For example, prompts for quick learners included advanced topics, while those for slower learners focused on fundamental concepts.

- Feedback Integration

  Used continuous feedback from students to refine prompts. This involved asking students about their understanding and comfort with the material and adjusting the difficulty and style of prompts accordingly.

■ Adaptive Learning Paths

Created adaptive learning paths that adjusted in real time based on student performance. This ensured that each student received personalized guidance that catered to their unique needs.

Outcome

■ Enhanced Engagement

Students became more engaged with the learning assistant, as the prompts were tailored to their individual needs and preferences.

■ Improved Educational Outcomes

There was a noticeable improvement in student performance and understanding of the material. Students reported finding the assistant more helpful and supportive.

■ Positive Feedback

The adaptability of the learning assistant was praised by both students and educators, highlighting its effectiveness in providing personalized learning experiences.

Example Prompts

■ Before

"What do you want to learn today?"

■ After

"Based on your recent progress, would you like to review quadratic equations or explore a new topic in algebra?"

These case studies highlight the transformative potential of advanced prompt engineering in creating effective and adaptive AI systems. By implementing dynamic prompts and integrating real-time data, the AI for disaster response coordination significantly improved its response times and accuracy, providing critical information efficiently during emergencies. Similarly, the personalized learning assistant demonstrated how tailored prompts based on individual performance data can enhance student engagement and educational outcomes.

These examples underscore the importance of continuous experimentation and refinement in prompt engineering. By understanding and addressing the specific needs of different contexts, AI developers can create systems that are both highly functional and deeply responsive to user requirements. This approach not only improves immediate interaction outcomes but also fosters long-term user satisfaction and trust.

TUTORIALS AND HANDS-ON EXERCISES

- Exercise 1 – Developing Adaptive Prompts for E-commerce
- Exercise 2 – Creating Effective Prompts for Customer Feedback Collection

Exercise 1 – Developing Adaptive Prompts for E-commerce

Exercise

Design prompts for an e-commerce chatbot that can adapt based on customer shopping behavior and preferences.

Steps

Step 1 – Analyze Typical Customer Interaction Patterns and Preferences

- Collect data on how customers interact with the e-commerce platform.
- Identify common behaviors, such as frequent searches, browsing history, and purchase patterns.
- Segment customers based on their preferences and shopping habits.

Step 2 – Create Prompts That Adjust Based on the Insights Gathered, Aiming to Personalize the Shopping Experience

- Develop a set of base prompts that can be customized according to customer segments.
- Create variations of these prompts tailored to different behaviors and preferences.

Example Prompts

- Frequent Buyer

  "Welcome back! Interested in checking out our new arrivals in [category]?"

- Bargain Hunter

  "Looking for great deals? Here are some products currently on sale."

- First-Time Visitor

  "Hi there! Can I help you find anything specific today? Here are some popular categories to get you started."

Step 3 – Test the Prompts with Simulated Customer Scenarios and Refine Based on Performance

- Use a simulation tool to create various customer scenarios and test the adaptive prompts.
- Gather data on how effectively the prompts engage customers and lead to desired outcomes (e.g., making a purchase, finding a product).
- Refine the prompts based on performance metrics such as user engagement, conversion rates, and feedback.

Exercise 2 – Creating Effective Prompts for Customer Feedback Collection

Exercise

Craft prompts are designed to elicit detailed and constructive feedback from users after a service interaction.

Steps

Step 1 – Identify Key Information Needed from Feedback to Improve Service

Determine the aspects of the service interaction that are most critical to improving user experience (e.g., response time, solution accuracy, agent friendliness).

Define the specific questions that will provide insights into these areas.

Step 2 – Design Prompts That Encourage Open and Detailed Responses Without Leading the User

Create neutral, open-ended prompts that allow users to share their experiences freely.

Ensure that the prompts do not suggest a particular type of response, which could bias the feedback.

Example Prompts

"Can you describe your overall experience with our customer service today?"

"What did you like most about your interaction with our support team?"

"Is there anything you think we could improve in our service?"

Step 3 – Implement and Evaluate the Effectiveness of These Prompts in a Live Environment

Integrate the feedback prompts into the post-interaction process of your service platform.

Monitor the quantity and quality of the feedback received.

Analyze the feedback to identify common themes and areas for improvement.

Adjust the prompts if necessary to improve the clarity or depth of the responses.

Example Implementation

After resolving a customer service inquiry, the chatbot or human agent can prompt the user with: "We value your feedback! Could you take a moment to tell us about your experience today?"

Evaluation Metrics

- Response Rate
  The percentage of users who provide feedback after an interaction.

- Feedback Quality
  The level of detail and constructiveness in the feedback received.

Actionable Insights

The extent to which the feedback provides clear directions for service improvement.

These hands-on exercises guide participants through the process of developing and refining adaptive prompts for specific applications, such as e-commerce and customer feedback collection. By analyzing customer behavior, personalizing interactions, and encouraging detailed feedback, these exercises help participants enhance their skills in crafting effective AI prompts. Through practical application and continuous refinement, participants can create AI systems that deliver personalized, responsive, and valuable interactions for users.

Prompts in Practice

Python Scripts

Sample code for creating and deploying adaptive prompts in various AI applications (see Figure 7.1).

```python
adaptive_prompt_personal_assistant.py > ...
1   from transformers import GPT2LMHeadModel, GPT2Tokenizer
2   import torch
3
4   # Load pre-trained model and tokenizer
5   model_name = 'gpt2'
6   model = GPT2LMHeadModel.from_pretrained(model_name)
7   tokenizer = GPT2Tokenizer.from_pretrained(model_name)
8
9   # Set the device to CUDA if available
10  device = torch.device('cuda' if torch.cuda.is_available() else 'cpu')
11  model.to(device)
12
13  # Function to determine context of user request
14  def determine_context(user_input):
15      if 'schedule' in user_input.lower() or 'appointment' in user_input.lower():
16          return 'schedule'
17      elif 'weather' in user_input.lower() or 'forecast' in user_input.lower():
18          return 'weather'
19      elif 'reminder' in user_input.lower() or 'remember' in user_input.lower():
20          return 'reminder'
21      else:
22          return 'general'
23
24  # Function to generate adaptive prompt based on context
25  def generate_adaptive_prompt(user_input):
26      context = determine_context(user_input)
27
28      if context == 'schedule':
29          prompt = f"Scheduling assistant: {user_input}"
30      elif context == 'weather':
31          prompt = f"Weather assistant: {user_input}"
32      elif context == 'reminder':
33          prompt = f"Reminder assistant: {user_input}"
```

FIGURE 7.1 Context-aware prompt generation with GPT.

Code Explanation: Context-Aware Prompt Generation with GPT-2

This script demonstrates how to create an adaptive AI assistant using the GPT-2 model from the Hugging Face Transformers library. The assistant tailors its responses based on the context of user inputs, such as scheduling, weather, or reminders. This approach highlights the importance of prompt engineering in generating contextually appropriate responses.

1. *Importing Libraries*

   The script starts by importing necessary components from the Transformers library and PyTorch:

   - *"GPT2LMHeadModel"* and *"GPT2Tokenizer"* from the Transformers library for loading the GPT-2 model and tokenizer.
   - *"torch"* for handling tensor operations and device management.

2. *Loading Pretrained Model and Tokenizer*

   The pretrained GPT-2 model and its tokenizer are loaded using the *"from_pretrained"* method with the model name *"gpt2"*. This initializes the model and tokenizer for use in generating text.

3. *Setting the Device to CUDA if Available*

   The script checks if CUDA (GPU) is available and sets the device accordingly:

   - *"torch.device("cuda"* if torch.cuda.is_available() else *"cpu")*: Selects GPU if available, otherwise defaults to CPU.
   - *"model.to(device)"*: Moves the model to the selected device for computation.

4. *"determine_context" Function*

   The *"determine_context"* function analyzes the user input to identify its context. It returns a context string based on specific keywords found in the input:

   - If the input contains words related to scheduling or appointments, it returns *"schedule"*.
   - If the input contains words related to weather or forecasts, it returns *"weather"*.
   - If the input contains words related to reminders or remembering, it returns *"reminder"*.
   - For all other inputs, it defaults to *"general"*.

5. *"generate_adaptive_prompt" Function*

   The *"generate_adaptive_prompt"* function creates a tailored prompt based on the context determined by the *"determine_context"* function:

   - Depending on the context, the function prefixes the user input with an appropriate assistant role (e.g., "Scheduling assistant:",

"Weather assistant:", "Reminder assistant:", or "Personal assistant:").

- This tailored prompt is then returned for further processing.

6. *"generate_response" Function*

The *"generate_response"* function generates a response based on the adaptive prompt:

- It tokenizes the prompt and converts it into tensor format, moving it to the selected device.
- The *"model.generate"* method is used to generate text up to a specified maximum length, with padding handled by the *"pad_ token_id"* set to the end-of-sequence token.
- The generated output is decoded back into human-readable text and returned.

Example Usage

An example user input is provided to demonstrate the entire process:

- The user input "Can you remind me to buy groceries tomorrow?" is passed to the *"generate_adaptive_prompt"* function to create a context-aware prompt.
- The adaptive prompt is then used to generate a response from the model.
- The script prints the original user input, the adaptive prompt, and the AI assistant's response.

Key Concepts for Prompt Engineering

- *Context Identification*: The script identifies the context of user inputs to tailor responses, highlighting the importance of understanding the user's intent in prompt engineering.
- *Adaptive Prompts*: By generating context-specific prompts, the script ensures that the AI assistant provides relevant and appropriate responses.
- *Device Management*: Efficiently using available hardware resources (CPU/GPU) for model inference.
- *Tokenization and Decoding*: Handling the conversion of text to and from tensor format for model processing and output generation.

Application in Prompt Engineering

In the context of prompt engineering, this script demonstrates several crucial techniques:

- *Contextual Relevance*: Tailoring prompts based on user input context ensures that responses are relevant and useful.
- *Adaptive Prompt Design*: Creating adaptive prompts based on context helps in fine-tuning the interaction quality and user experience.
- *Dynamic Response Generation*: Leveraging model capabilities to generate responses dynamically based on varying prompts and contexts.

Datasets

Customer Interaction Logs

A dataset containing examples of customer interactions across multiple industries, useful for training and testing prompt designs.

Example from dataset:

```
[
    {
        "interaction_id": "c001",
        "timestamp": "2024-06-01T10:15:30Z",
        "industry": "Retail",
        "user_id": "u001",
        "interaction_type": "query",
        "user_input": "I'd like to know the status of
my order.",
        "ai_response": "Your order is currently being
processed and will be shipped within 2 days."
    },
    {
        "interaction_id": "c002",
        "timestamp": "2024-06-01T11:20:45Z",
        "industry": "Telecommunications",
        "user_id": "u002",
```

```
        "interaction_type": "complaint",
        "user_input": "My internet connection is very
slow.",
        "ai_response": "I'm sorry for the inconvenience.
Let me run a diagnostic test on your connection."
    },
```

Educational Data

Access to a dataset of student learning interactions, ideal for developing personalized educational AI tools.

Example from dataset:

```
[
    {
        "interaction_id": "e001",
        "timestamp": "2024-06-01T10:30:00Z",
        "student_id": "s001",
        "interaction_type": "question",
        "subject": "Mathematics",
        "student_input": "Can you help me solve this
algebra problem?",
        "ai_response": "Sure, let's start by identifying
the variables in the equation."
    },
    {
        "interaction_id": "e002",
        "timestamp": "2024-06-01T11:45:20Z",
        "student_id": "s002",
        "interaction_type": "feedback",
        "subject": "History",
        "student_input": "I found the lesson on World
War II very informative.",
        "ai_response": "I'm glad you enjoyed it! Is
there a specific topic you'd like to explore further?"
    },
```

CONCLUSION

Chapter 7 has provided a crucial bridge between theoretical under-standing and practical application in the field of prompt engineering. By engaging with hands-on exercises and analyzing real-world case studies, readers have gained invaluable insights into the practical implementa-tion of advanced prompt engineering techniques.

Key Takeaways

Practical Application of Techniques

The hands-on exercises have demonstrated how to design, test, and refine prompts for various AI applications. From developing adaptive prompts for e-commerce chatbots to creating effective prompts for cus-tomer feedback collection, these exercises have equipped readers with the skills needed to enhance AI interactions in real-world scenarios.

Real-World Case Studies

The case studies have highlighted successful implementations of prompt engineering across different domains. By examining examples such as AI for disaster response coordination and personalized learn-ing assistants, readers have seen the tangible benefits of well-crafted prompts in improving user engagement, satisfaction, and overall system effectiveness.

Encouragement of Experimentation

This chapter has emphasized the importance of continuous experimen-tation and iteration in prompt engineering. By varying prompt styles, testing contextual flexibility, and incorporating user feedback, readers have learned how subtle changes can significantly impact AI behavior and interaction quality.

Reflecting on the Exercises

Adaptive E-commerce Prompts

Through exercises in developing adaptive prompts for e-commerce, readers have learned to personalize the shopping experience based on customer behavior and preferences. This skill is essential for increasing user engagement and driving sales.

Effective Feedback Collection

Crafting prompts to elicit detailed and constructive feedback has shown readers how to gather valuable insights for service improvement. The ability to design such prompts ensures that AI systems can continuously evolve based on user needs and expectations.

Analyzing Case Studies

Disaster Response Coordination

The case study on disaster response highlighted how dynamic prompts and real-time data integration can enhance the responsiveness and accuracy of AI systems in critical situations.

Personalized Learning Assistants

The personalized learning assistant case study demonstrated the power of tailored prompts in adapting to individual learning preferences and improving educational outcomes.

Looking Ahead

The insights and skills gained from this chapter are not just applicable to the scenarios presented but are transferable to a wide range of AI applications. As AI technology continues to advance, the ability to craft effective and adaptive prompts will remain a cornerstone of successful AI development.

By mastering the techniques covered in this chapter, readers are well-equipped to tackle complex AI challenges, drive innovation, and create user-centric AI systems that excel in diverse real-world contexts. This practical foundation, combined with a mindset of continuous improvement and experimentation, ensures that readers can contribute to the cutting-edge of AI prompt engineering and deliver impactful, high-quality AI solutions.

In summary, Chapter 7 reinforced the importance of hands-on practice and real-world application in mastering prompt engineering. Through exercises and case studies, readers have developed a deeper understanding of how to create sophisticated, effective, and user-friendly AI systems. This knowledge positions them to innovate and excel in the dynamic field of AI, driving forward the capabilities and potential of conversational AI technologies.

BEST PRACTICES AND FUTURE DIRECTIONS

As the field of artificial intelligence continues to advance at a rapid pace, the importance of robust prompt engineering practices cannot be overstated. Chapter 8 focuses on consolidating the essential best practices discussed throughout this book while looking forward to emerging trends and future directions in conversational AI. This chapter aims to equip readers with a comprehensive understanding of the most effective strategies for prompt engineering and to foster an environment of continuous improvement and innovation.

KEY OBJECTIVES

Review of Best Practices

Summarize the essential best practices for prompt engineering that have been covered in previous chapters.

Highlight the importance of clarity, precision, contextual relevance, iterative testing, and ethical considerations in prompt design.

Exploration of Recent Advancements

Discuss the latest advancements in natural language understanding (NLU), personalization techniques, and AI ethics and governance.

Provide insights into how these advancements are shaping the future of conversational AI and prompt engineering.

Encouragement of Experimentation and Discussion

Emphasize the value of fostering a collaborative and experimental mindset among practitioners.

Suggest strategies for engaging with the AI community, contributing to open-source projects, and staying informed about ongoing research and technological breakthroughs.

Structure of the Chapter

Review of Essential Best Practices

This section will consolidate the key best practices discussed throughout the book, providing a clear and concise summary of the most effective strategies for prompt engineering.

Recent Advancements and Emerging Trends

Explore the latest research and trends in conversational AI, including advancements in NLU, personalization, and ethical AI practices. This section will highlight how these developments are influencing prompt engineering techniques.

Fostering Continuous Improvement

Discuss strategies for fostering an environment of continuous experimentation and discussion, emphasizing the importance of community engagement, open-source contributions, and continual learning.

Future Directions

Offer a forward-looking perspective on the potential future developments in conversational AI and prompt engineering, encouraging readers to stay innovative and adaptive in their practices.

Key Topics Covered

- *Clarity and Precision in Prompt Design*

  Ensure prompts are clear and precise to reduce ambiguity and enhance AI performance.

- *Contextual Relevance*

  Maintain the relevance of prompts to the specific context and purpose of the interaction.

- *Iterative Testing and Refinement*

  Continuously test and refine prompts based on feedback and performance metrics to improve outcomes.

- *Ethical Considerations*

  Incorporate ethical guidelines in the design of prompts to prevent biases and ensure fairness.

- *Advancements in Natural Language Understanding (NLU)*

  Discuss recent improvements in AI's ability to understand human language more deeply and contextually.

- *Personalization Techniques*

  Develop more sophisticated methods for personalizing AI responses based on user history and preferences.

- *AI Ethics and Governance*

  Highlight the increasing focus on developing frameworks and guidelines for ethical AI practices.

- *Community Engagement and Open-Source Contributions*

  Encourage participation in forums, workshops, and open-source projects to exchange ideas and collaborate on new techniques.

- *Continual Learning*

  Emphasize the importance of staying informed about the latest research, case studies, and technological breakthroughs.

By the end of this chapter, readers will have a consolidated understanding of the best practices for prompt engineering and be well-prepared to engage with emerging trends and future developments in conversational AI. This comprehensive approach ensures that practitioners are equipped to create sophisticated, user-centric AI systems that are both effective and ethically sound.

REVIEW OF ESSENTIAL BEST PRACTICES AND KEY TAKEAWAYS FROM THE BOOK

Highlighting the best practices and consolidating the key insights from the book help ensure that readers can effectively apply prompt engineering techniques to develop sophisticated, user-friendly AI systems.

Best Practices

Clarity and Precision in Prompt Design

Importance

Clear and precise prompts reduce ambiguity, ensuring that the AI interprets and responds accurately to user inputs.

Implementation

Use straightforward language and specific instructions to guide the AI effectively.

Example

Instead of "Tell me more," use "Please provide details about the product's features."

Contextual Relevance

Importance

Prompts must be relevant to the specific context and purpose of the interaction to maintain user engagement and satisfaction.

Implementation

Incorporate contextual cues and background information to tailor prompts to the user's current situation.

Example

"Based on your recent purchase of a laptop, would you like to know about compatible accessories?"

Iterative Testing and Refinement

Importance

Continuously testing and refining prompts based on feedback and performance metrics helps improve AI outcomes over time.

Implementation

Regularly evaluate prompt effectiveness through user feedback and performance data, adjusting as needed.

Example

A/B testing different prompts to determine which version yields better user satisfaction and accuracy.

Ethical Considerations

Importance

Incorporating ethical guidelines in prompt design is essential to prevent biases and ensure fairness, transparency, and accountability in AI interactions.

Implementation

Design prompts that are inclusive and considerate of diverse user backgrounds and perspectives.

Example

Avoiding biased language and ensuring prompts are respectful and inclusive for all users.

Key Takeaways

Effective Prompt Engineering Enhances AI Performance

Well-crafted prompts significantly improve the accuracy, relevance, and overall utility of AI systems, leading to better user experiences and outcomes.

Understanding Prompt Components

A thorough understanding of the components of a prompt (instructions, context, and user input) and how they interact is crucial for successful AI interactions.

Example components include clear instructions, contextual information, and specific user input requirements.

Continuous Learning and Adaptation

Staying updated with rapid advancements in AI technology is essential for maintaining and enhancing AI systems. Continuous learning and adaptation ensure that AI remains effective and relevant.

Engaging in ongoing education, experimentation, and refinement of prompt engineering practices is necessary to keep pace with technological developments.

Integration of Ethical Practices

Ethical considerations are integral to prompt engineering, ensuring that AI systems operate fairly and do not perpetuate existing biases or inequalities.

Example practices include regular audits for bias, incorporating diverse perspectives in prompt design, and maintaining transparency in AI decision-making processes.

The book has provided a comprehensive guide to prompt engineering, emphasizing the importance of clarity, contextual relevance, iterative refinement, and ethical considerations. By mastering these best practices and key insights, readers can develop highly effective and user-friendly AI systems.

Effective prompt engineering is foundational to enhancing the performance and utility of AI. Understanding the components of a prompt and continuously adapting to advancements in AI technology are essential for creating successful AI interactions. Ethical considerations must be integrated into every step of the prompt engineering process to ensure fairness and inclusivity.

By applying these best practices and key takeaways, readers are well-equipped to innovate and excel in the dynamic field of AI prompt engineering, driving forward the capabilities and potential of conversational AI technologies.

DISCUSSION OF ONGOING RESEARCH, RECENT ADVANCEMENTS, AND EMERGING TRENDS IN CONVERSATIONAL AI AND PROMPT ENGINEERING

Exploring the latest research and trends is crucial for practitioners to stay informed and prepared for future developments in conversational AI and prompt engineering. This section provides an overview of recent advancements, emerging trends, and ongoing research in the field.

Recent Advancements and Trends

Advancements in Natural Language Understanding (NLU)

Overview

Considerable progress has been made in the field of NLU, enabling AI systems to comprehend human language more deeply and contextually. This includes understanding nuanced meanings, detecting sentiments, and recognizing intents more accurately.

Key Developments

Transformers and BERT Models

The introduction of transformer-based models like BERT (Bidirectional Encoder Representations from Transformers) has revolutionized NLU by providing a deeper understanding of context and meaning in text.

Contextual AI

Improvements in contextual AI allow systems to maintain context across longer conversations, resulting in more coherent and relevant responses.

Impact on Prompt Engineering

These advancements enable more precise and context-aware prompt designs, enhancing the effectiveness of conversational AI interactions.

Personalization Techniques

Overview

Personalization in AI involves tailoring responses based on individual user history, preferences, and behaviors. This trend is becoming increasingly sophisticated, enabling more engaging and relevant user experiences.

Key Developments

User Profiling

Advanced techniques for creating detailed user profiles based on past interactions and behaviors.

Adaptive Learning

AI systems that adapt in real time to user feedback and changing preferences.

Impact on Prompt Engineering

Personalized prompts can significantly improve user satisfaction by making interactions feel more tailored and responsive. This requires designing prompts that can dynamically adjust based on user data.

AI Ethics and Governance

Overview

As AI systems become more pervasive, there is a growing emphasis on ensuring they operate ethically and fairly. This involves developing frameworks and guidelines to govern AI practices, addressing issues such as bias, transparency, and accountability.

Key Developments

Ethical AI Frameworks

Organizations and researchers are developing comprehensive frameworks to guide the ethical use of AI, including principles for fairness, transparency, and accountability.

Bias Detection and Mitigation

Techniques to detect and mitigate biases in AI models, ensuring more equitable outcomes.

Impact on Prompt Engineering

Ethical considerations must be integrated into prompt design to prevent biases and ensure fairness. This includes regular audits, diverse testing groups, and transparent prompt engineering practices.

Ongoing Research Areas

Multimodal AI

Overview

Research is expanding into multimodal AI, which integrates multiple types of data (e.g., text, images, audio) to enhance understanding and response capabilities.

Implications

Multimodal AI can lead to more comprehensive and nuanced interactions, requiring prompt engineering to accommodate and leverage multiple data types.

Explainable AI (XAI)

Overview

Explainable AI aims to make AI systems more transparent and understandable to users. This includes developing methods to explain how AI arrives at its decisions.

Implications

Prompts may need to include explanations or justifications for AI responses, especially in high-stakes applications like healthcare and finance.

Human–AI Collaboration

Overview

Research is focusing on how AI can effectively collaborate with humans, augmenting human capabilities rather than replacing them.

Implications

Prompt engineering must facilitate seamless human–AI collaboration, designing prompts that support and enhance human decision-making.

Low-Resource Languages

Overview

Efforts are being made to improve AI capabilities in low-resource languages, expanding the reach and accessibility of AI technologies.

Implications

Designing prompts for diverse linguistic and cultural contexts to ensure inclusivity and effectiveness across different user groups.

Keeping abreast of ongoing research, recent advancements, and emerging trends is essential for practitioners in the field of conversational

AI and prompt engineering. Advances in NLU, personalization techniques, and AI ethics are driving the evolution of AI capabilities, while ongoing research in multimodal AI, explainable AI, human–AI collaboration, and low-resource languages is shaping the future landscape.

By staying informed about these developments, practitioners can better prepare for future challenges and opportunities, ensuring their AI systems are not only effective but also ethical and inclusive. This continuous learning and adaptation are critical for maintaining the forefront of AI technology and delivering high-quality, user-centric AI interactions.

FOSTERING AN ENVIRONMENT FOR FURTHER EXPERIMENTATION AND DISCUSSION ON OPTIMIZING PROMPT ENGINEERING PRACTICES

Encouraging an ongoing dialogue among practitioners, researchers, and enthusiasts helps propel the field forward and fosters a community of continuous improvement. By engaging in collaborative efforts and sharing knowledge, the AI community can drive innovation and enhance the effectiveness of prompt engineering practices.

Strategies for Fostering Experimentation

Community Engagement

Importance

Engaging with the broader AI community provides opportunities for knowledge exchange, collaboration, and inspiration.

Implementation

Forums and Online Communities

Participate in forums like Reddit's AI communities, Stack Overflow, and specialized AI forums to discuss challenges and share solutions.

Workshops and Meetups

Attend or organize local and virtual workshops, meetups, and hackathons to collaborate on projects and learn from peers.

Conferences and Seminars

Join AI conferences and seminars to stay updated on the latest research and network with experts in the field.

Example

Participate in conferences like NeurIPS, ICML, and ACL to gain insights into innovative AI research and developments.

Open-Source Contributions

Importance

Contributing to open-source projects fosters collaboration and accelerates innovation by leveraging collective expertise and resources.

Implementation

Contribute to Projects

Actively contribute to open-source AI projects on platforms like GitHub and GitLab. Share your prompt engineering techniques and improvements with the community.

Utilize Open Source

Tools

Use open-source libraries and tools to build and refine AI systems, benefiting from the collective advancements made by the community.

Collaborative Development

Engage in collaborative development efforts, working with others to enhance and expand the capabilities of existing open-source projects.

Example

Contribute to open-source projects like OpenAI's GPT-3, Hugging Face Transformers, or TensorFlow to help advance prompt engineering techniques.

Continual Learning

Importance

Staying informed about the latest research, case studies, and technological breakthroughs is essential for continuous improvement and
innovation.

Implementation

Research Papers and Journals

Regularly read AI research papers and journals to keep up with new
findings and methodologies. Platforms like arXiv, Google Scholar, and
ResearchGate are valuable resources.

Online Courses and Tutorials

Enroll in online courses, webinars, and tutorials to learn new skills and
techniques. Websites like Coursera, edX, and Udacity offer AI and
machine learning courses.

Case Studies and Whitepapers

Study case studies and whitepapers from industry leaders to understand
real-world applications and the impact of various prompt engineering
strategies.

Example

Enroll in courses such as Stanford's CS224N (Natural Language
Processing with Deep Learning) or Andrew Ng's Deep Learning
Specialization on Coursera to deepen your understanding of AI and
prompt engineering.

Fostering an environment of continuous experimentation and discussion is vital for the advancement of prompt engineering practices. By
engaging with the AI community, contributing to open-source projects,
and committing to continual learning, practitioners can drive innovation and enhance the effectiveness of AI systems.

Key Takeaways

- *Community Engagement*
  Actively participating in forums, workshops, and conferences facilitates knowledge exchange and collaboration.

▪ *Open-Source Contributions*

Contributing to and utilizing open-source projects harnesses collective expertise and resources.

▪ *Continual Learning*

Staying informed about the latest research and technological breakthroughs ensures ongoing improvement and adaptation.

By implementing these strategies, practitioners can create a dynamic and collaborative ecosystem that supports the continuous evolution of prompt engineering techniques. This collective effort not only propels the field forward but also ensures that AI systems remain at the forefront of technological advancements, delivering increasingly sophisticated and user-centric interactions.

CONCLUSION

Chapter 8 has provided a comprehensive synthesis of the best practices in prompt engineering, while also looking ahead to the future of conversational AI. By consolidating essential strategies and exploring recent advancements, this chapter equips readers with the knowledge and tools necessary to excel in the dynamic field of AI development.

Key Takeaways

Clarity and Precision in Prompt Design

Ensuring that prompts are clear and precise is fundamental to reducing ambiguity and enhancing AI performance. This practice helps create more reliable and accurate AI interactions.

Contextual Relevance

Maintaining the relevance of prompts to the specific context and purpose of the interaction ensures that AI responses are appropriate and effective. Contextual awareness is crucial for meeting user needs and expectations.

Iterative Testing and Refinement

Continuous testing and refinement based on user feedback and performance metrics are essential for improving AI outcomes. This iterative approach allows for constant improvement and adaptation to changing requirements.

Ethical Considerations

Integrating ethical guidelines into prompt design helps prevent biases and ensures fairness in AI systems. Ethical prompt engineering fosters trust and accountability, which are vital for long-term success.

Recent Advancements and Emerging Trends

Advancements in Natural Language Understanding (NLU)

Significant improvements in AI's ability to understand human language more deeply and contextually have transformed conversational AI. Leveraging these advancements can enhance the sophistication and accuracy of AI systems.

Personalization Techniques

Developing sophisticated methods for personalizing AI responses based on user history and preferences leads to more engaging and relevant interactions. Personalization is key to user satisfaction and loyalty.

AI Ethics and Governance

The increasing focus on ethical AI practices and governance frameworks ensures that AI systems operate fairly and transparently. Staying informed about these developments is crucial for responsible AI development.

Fostering Continuous Improvement

Community Engagement

Engaging with the AI community through forums, workshops, and conferences facilitates knowledge exchange and collaboration. Building a network of peers and experts can drive innovation and support continuous learning.

Open-Source Contributions

Contributing to and utilizing open-source projects harnesses collective expertise and resources. Open-source collaboration accelerates the development and refinement of AI technologies.

Continual Learning

Staying informed about the latest research, case studies, and techno-logical breakthroughs is essential for maintaining the forefront of AI development. Continuous education and experimentation are key to adapting to rapid advancements.

Future Directions

As the field of conversational AI continues to evolve, practitioners must remain initiative-taking in adopting modern technologies and meth-odologies. Emerging trends in multimodal AI, explainable AI (XAI), human–AI collaboration, and support for low-resource languages are shaping the future landscape. By staying engaged with ongoing research and fostering a culture of continuous improvement, AI developers can create more effective, ethical, and user-centric systems.

Final Thoughts

The knowledge and practices outlined in this book provide a robust foundation for mastering prompt engineering. By adhering to best practices, staying informed about advancements, and engaging with the AI community, practitioners can drive the development of sophis-ticated AI systems that deliver high-quality, user-friendly interactions. The journey of prompt engineering is one of continuous learning and adaptation, ensuring that AI technologies remain innovative, ethical, and impactful in addressing the needs of diverse users.

INDEX

Introduction

This guide walks you through the installation and configuration of Office Web Apps Server integrated with SharePoint 2013. Both Windows Server 2008 R2 and Windows Server 2012 installations are explored.

Reference links and source code are available on www.stevethemanmann.com:

Installing and Configuring Office Web Apps Server in SharePoint 2013

Copyright © 2013 by Steven Mann

Trademarks

Screenshots of Microsoft Products and Services

Warning and Disclaimer

Volume 6

Installing and Configuring Office Web Apps Server in SharePoint 2013

STEVEN MANN

SharePoint 2013
Solution Series
Volumes 6-10

Step 1A: Prepare for Office Web Apps Server on Windows Server 2008 R2

If you are using Windows Server 2008 R2, you need to make sure the following is installed first:

- Windows Server 2008 R2 Service Pack 1
- .NET Framework 4.5
- Windows PowerShell 3.0
- KB2592525

Add the required server features using PowerShell:

```
Import-Module ServerManager


Add-WindowsFeature Web-Server,Web-WebServer,Web-
Common-Http,Web-Static-Content,Web-App-Dev,Web-Asp-
Net,Web-Net-Ext,Web-ISAPI-Ext,Web-ISAPI-Filter,Web-
Includes,Web-Security,Web-Windows-Auth,Web-
Filtering,Web-Stat-Compression,Web-Dyn-
Compression,Web-Mgmt-Console,Ink-Handwriting,IH-Ink-
Support
```

If the output shows that a restart is needed (Restart Needed = Yes), restart your server before continuing.

Step 1B: Prepare for Office Web Apps Server on Windows Server 2012

Preparing your server on Windows Server 2012 is slightly different. You need to add the features as follows:

Import-Module ServerManager

Add-WindowsFeature Web-Server,Web-Mgmt-Tools,Web-Mgmt-Console,Web-WebServer,Web-Common-Http,Web-Default-Doc,Web-Static-Content,Web-Performance,Web-Stat-Compression,Web-Dyn-Compression,Web-Security,Web-Filtering,Web-Windows-Auth,Web-App-Dev,Web-Net-Ext45,Web-Asp-Net45,Web-ISAPI-Ext,Web-ISAPI-Filter,Web-Includes,InkandHandwritingServices

If the output shows that a restart is needed, restart your server before continuing.

Step 2: Download and Install Office Web Apps Server 2013 (October 2012 Release)

Download and install the Office Web Apps Server 2013 October 2013 Release (http://www.microsoft.com/en-us/download/details.aspx?id=35489)

Step 3: Download and Install Office Web Apps Server 2013 Public Update (March 2013 Update)

Next, download and install the Office Web Apps Server update located at: http://www.microsoft.com/en-us/download/details.aspx?id=36981

Step 4: Create the Office Web Apps Farm

Now you need to create the new Office Web Apps Farm on the server via PowerShell:

```
Import-Module OfficeWebApps

New-OfficeWebAppsFarm -InternalURL http://servername
-AllowHttp -EditingEnabled
```

```
Administrator: Windows PowerShell                                        _ □ ×
Windows PowerShell
Copyright (C) 2012 Microsoft Corporation. All rights reserved.

PS F:\> Import-Module OfficeWebApps
PS F:\> New-OfficeWebAppsFarm -InternalURL http://stvspsm13 -AllowHttp -EditingEnabled
_
```

Confirm the Editing operation:

```
Setting EditingEnabled to TRUE. You should only do this if users of this Office Web Apps Server have licenses that
permit editing using Office Web Apps.
Continue with this operation?
[Y] Yes  [N] No  [S] Suspend  [?] Help (default is "Y"): y
_
```

The operation results with all of the properties displayed:

```
FarmOU                         :
InternalURL                    : http://stvspsm13/
ExternalURL                    :
AllowHTTP                      : True
SSLOffloaded                   : False
CertificateName                :
EditingEnabled                 : True
LogLocation                    : C:\ProgramData\Microsoft\OfficeWebApps\Data\Logs\ULS
LogRetentionInDays             : 7
LogVerbosity                   :
Proxy                          :
CacheLocation                  : C:\ProgramData\Microsoft\OfficeWebApps\Working\d
MaxMemoryCacheSizeInMB         : 75
DocumentInfoCacheSize          : 5000
CacheSizeInGB                  : 15
ClipartEnabled                 : False
TranslationEnabled             : False
MaxTranslationCharacterCount   : 125000
TranslationServiceAppId        :
TranslationServiceAddress      :
RenderingLocalCacheLocation    : C:\ProgramData\Microsoft\OfficeWebApps\Working\waccache
RecycleActiveProcessCount      : 5
AllowCEIP                      : False
ExcelRequestDurationMax        : 300
ExcelSessionTimeout            : 450
ExcelWorkbookSizeMax           : 10
ExcelPrivateBytesMax           : -1
ExcelConnectionLifetime        : 1800
ExcelExternalDataCacheLifetime : 300
ExcelAllowExternalData         : True
ExcelWarnOnDataRefresh         : True
OpenFromUrlEnabled             : False
OpenFromUncEnabled             : True
OpenFromUrlThrottlingEnabled   : True
AllowHttpSecureStoreConnections: False
Machines                       : {STVSPSM13}
```

The next step is to test the Office Web Apps server using a browser to confirm that http://servername/hosting/discovery produces a wopi-discovery response:

Now onto the SharePoint 2013 Farm!

Step 5: Bind SharePoint 2013 to Office Web Apps

Open the SharePoint 2013 Management Shell on one of your farm servers. Create the new binding using the following command:

New-SPWOPIBinding -ServerName <WacServerName> -AllowHTTP

Set the zone:

```
Set-SPWopiZone -zone "internal-http"
```

If you are using HTTP, you need to allow OAuth over HTTP by using the following commands:

$config = (Get-SPSecurityTokenServiceConfig)
$config.AllowOAuthOverHttp = $true
$config.Update()

Step 6: Verify SharePoint 2013 is Using Office Web Apps

Browse a document library with Office documents:

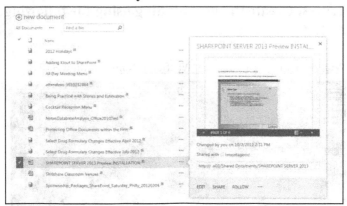

Search for Office documents: (may need to perform a full crawl before the preview kicks in)

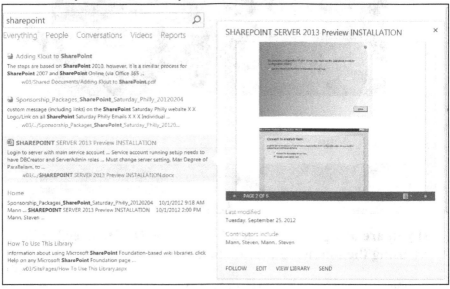

Conclusion

This guide walked through the steps to install and configure Office Web Apps Server for SharePoint 2013. It is surprising at times how easy it is to install and configure Office Web Apps Server in SharePoint 2013. I hope you found this guide useful and informative.

Volume 7

How to Enhance PDF Results and Previews in SharePoint 2013 Search

STEVEN MANN

How to Enhance PDF Results and Previews in SharePoint 2013 Search

Copyright © 2013 by Steven Mann

Trademarks

Screenshots of Microsoft Products and Services

Warning and Disclaimer

Introduction

This guide discusses the behaviors of PDF Document search results in SharePoint 2013 as well as various preview options. PDF Document Previews in search results are possible both with and without Office Web Apps Server 2013. This guide walks through both options and demonstrates a hybrid approach as well.

Reference links and source code is available on www.stevethemanmann.com:

PDF Handling Overview

SharePoint 2013 supports PDF documents out-of-the-box. Initially, web applications do not allow opening PDFs in the browser, however, by adding PDF as an allowed MIME type, browser rendering via Adobe is achieved.

Office Web Apps server provides Office document previews and rendering in Search results without the need for client applications installed (e.g. Word, Excel, etc.). However, once SharePoint is bound to Office Web Apps, PDF documents no longer open in the browser.

There are two workarounds –

1) Configure PDF items to render as Word Items which allows PDFs to open and preview in Search within Office Web Apps

2) Modify the PDF Item display template which allows PDFs to render in the browser via Adobe. Modify the PDF hover template to display previews.

These workarounds take care of Search, but PDFs will still open in the client application (e.g. Adobe) from Document Libraries. The solution here is an update to Office Web Apps. The February/March 2013 Update to Office Web Apps server supports opening PDFs from document libraries within Office Web Apps.

The following table summarizes the various PDF rendering and preview behaviors:

	Search PDF Preview	Search Open (clicking on result)	Document Library Open (clicking on Document)
Out of the Box (Strict Web App)	Available by modifying the Display Template	Opens in Adobe or associated client application	Opens in Adobe or associated client application
Out of the Box (Permissive Web App or Allowed Mime Type of PDF)	Available by modifying the Display Template	Opens in web browser and search term is passed into Adobe	Web Browser
Office Web Apps Server (October 2012 Release)	Two options: 1. Display template (shows in Adobe web) 2. Modify Result Type to use Word Item (shows in Word App Web)	Opens in Adobe or associated client application. Opens in Browser with modification of display template	Opens in Adobe or associated client application.
Office Web Apps Server (Feb/Mar 2013 Update)	Two options: 1. Display template (shows in Adobe web) 2. Modify Result Type to use Word Item (shows in Word App Web)	Opens in browser using Word Web App. Can use templates to display in Adobe Web.	Opens in browser using Word Web App. If not bound to WordPDF – Opens in Adobe or associated client application.

It is also worth mentioning that if Office Web Apps is not used for Search results of PDFs, the opening of PDFs in the browser passes the search terms into Adobe and thus finds the occurrences within the document. An example of this "search term pass-through" is displayed below:

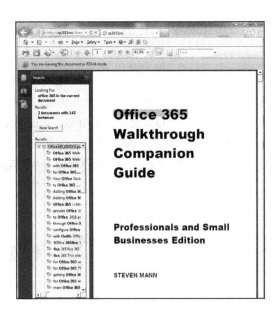

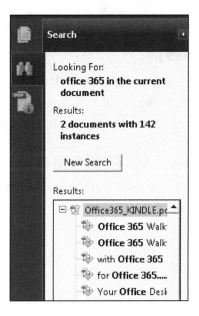

Based on my investigations and modifications, when using Office Web Apps server with SharePoint, there are two overall options when handling PDFs. One provides a more consistent user experience and the other provides the most functionality.

Most Consistent User Experience

The most consistent user experience would be to use Office Web Apps server (with the update) to enable opening of PDFs from libraries in the browser and to modify the search result type to render PDFs as Word Items which enables both preview and opening of the documents from Search results within Office Web Apps.

Most Functionality

The option that provides the most functionality is to use Office Web Apps for document libraries such that PDFs are opened within the browser but then use customized search templates to preview and open PDFs from Search results thus providing the search term pass-through functionality as described above. For the most consistent preview, use a customized copy of the Word item hover panel template.

The rest of this guide steps through the details and explains how to accomplish the various options and behaviors.

PDF Handling Out-Of-The-Box (without Office Web Apps Server)

Web Applications are created with the Browser File Handling option set to Strict. This means that only the default allowed MIME types (correlates to document types such Word, PDF, etc.) can open and display within the browser without prompting the user to Open or Save the document. PDF is not one of those default MIME types and thus, the user is prompted when attempting to open a PDF document:

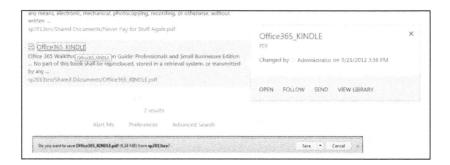

The recommended way to enable PDFs to be opened in the browser is to add the MIME type to the allowed list of types by using PowerShell commands:

```
$webApplication = Get-SPWebApplication "http:/yourwebapplicationurl"
$webAppApplication.AllowedInlineDownloadedMimeTypes.Add("application/pdf")
$webApplication.Update()
```

Source:
http://social.technet.microsoft.com/wiki/contents/articles/8073.sharepoint-2010-and-2013-browser-file-handling-deep-dive.aspx#DownloadFunctions

The other easy option, which is not recommended, is to modify your web application (via Central Admin) and change the Browser File Handling property to Permissive:

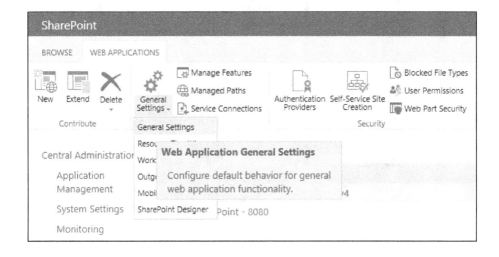

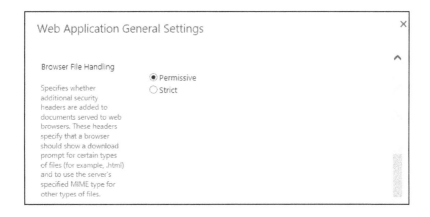

Either method will allow PDF files to be opened in the browser. A neat experience in search results is that the search term is passed into Adobe and the terms are highlighted in the document:

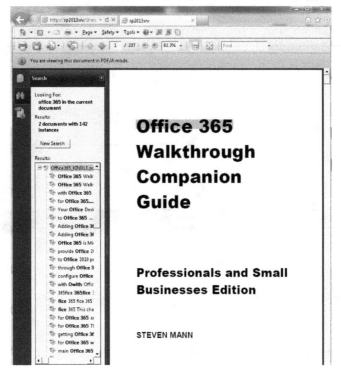

PDF Handling with Office Web Apps October 2012 Release Version

Once Office Web Apps is installed and configured, by surprise, PDF documents no longer open in the browser. Neither from document libraries nor from the search results. So there two options at this point (at least for the search results).

1. Copy the PDF Result Type and use the Word Item template for PDFs. This method both shows a preview and opens up PDF search results in the Office Web App's Word App Viewer. (See section in this guide for steps).

2. Use my original method for creating a PDF Preview to generate the preview by modifying the Display Templates. (See section in this guide for the steps).

Follow these steps to allow opening of the PDF document in the browser via Adobe (maintaining the search term pass-through functionality:

Modify the Item_PDF.html in the display templates folder. (see next sections for detailed steps on how to get to the templates)

Replace this line:

ctx.CurrentItem.csr_OpenControl = "PdfFile.OpenDocuments";

With this one:

ctx.CurrentItem.csr_OpenApp = "word";

```
if(!Srch.U.e(k)){
    ctx.CurrentItem.csr_Path = ctx.CurrentItem.Path + "#search=" + $urlKeyValueEncode(k);
}
ctx.CurrentItem.csr_Icon = Srch.U.getIconUrlByFileExtension(ctx.CurrentItem);
ctx.CurrentItem.csr_OpenControl = "PdfFile.OpenDocuments";
ctx.currentItem_ShowHoverPanelCallback = Srch.U.getShowHoverPanelCallback(itemId, hoverId, hoverUrl);
ctx.currentItem_HideHoverPanelCallback = Srch.U.getHideHoverPanelCallback();
```

```
if(!Srch.U.e(k)){
    ctx.CurrentItem.csr_Path = ctx.CurrentItem.Path + "#search=" + $urlKeyValueEncode(k);
}
ctx.CurrentItem.csr_Icon = Srch.U.getIconUrlByFileExtension(ctx.CurrentItem);
ctx.CurrentItem.csr_OpenApp = "word";
ctx.currentItem_ShowHoverPanelCallback = Srch.U.getShowHoverPanelCallback(itemId, hoverId, hoverUrl);
ctx.currentItem_HideHoverPanelCallback = Srch.U.getHideHoverPanelCallback();
```

Problems solved, right? At this point the search is fixed but PDFs
don't open from document libraries in the browser. That's where
the Office Web Apps Update comes in to play!

PDF Handling with Office Web Apps Server Public Update (March 2013) using a Hybrid Approach

There was a cumulative and public update released in early March 2013 that adds additional support for PDFs in SharePoint 2013 using Office Web Apps server. The update adds a new application type named WordPDF. It allows PDFs to be opened from document libraries in the browser using the Word App Viewer.

What about search? For search, there is no change. You either need to copy the PDF Result Type and configure it to use the Word Item or modify the search display templates. (Same options as above).

However, I have come up with a hybrid approach that provides a consistent preview using the Word App Viewer but also provides the rendering of PDFs in the browser through Adobe with the search term pass-through!

Fire up SharePoint Designer 2013 and Open the Search Center Site

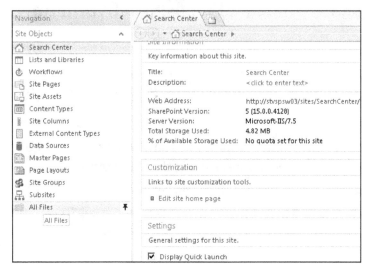

Click on All Files from the left-hand navigation

If you attempt to get the files from the Master Pages, you will not see any items once you get to the Display Templates folders.

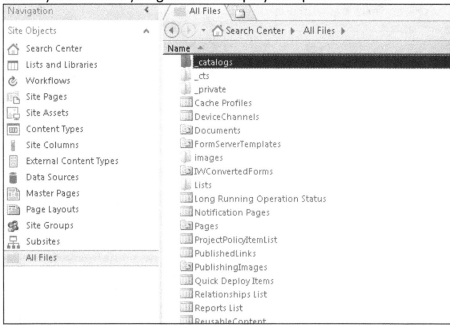

You see the list of all files in the main window.

Double-click on the _catalogs folder in the main window

This action displays the _catalogs structure under the left-hand navigation.

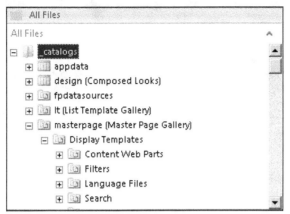

Expand the _catalogs folder, then the masterpage folder, and then the Display Templates folder.

Click on the Search folder under Display Templates

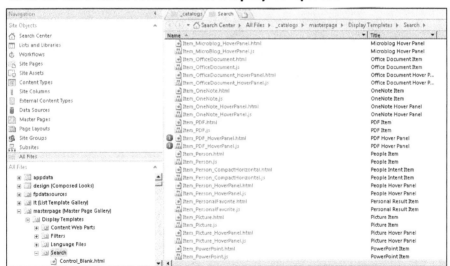

Find Item_PDF.html. Right-click and select Copy:

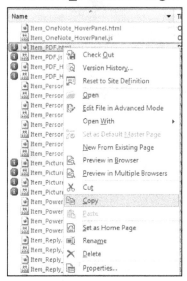

Right-click again and select Paste:

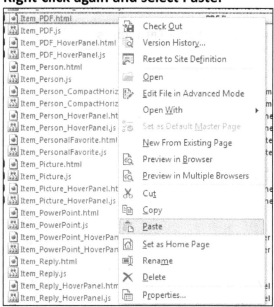

This process creates a copy of the file which appears at the bottom of the list. Find the copy and rename to something different (such as Item_PDFCustom.html):

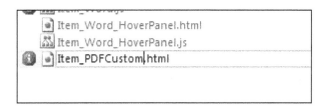

Right-click the new file and select Edit File in Advanced Mode:

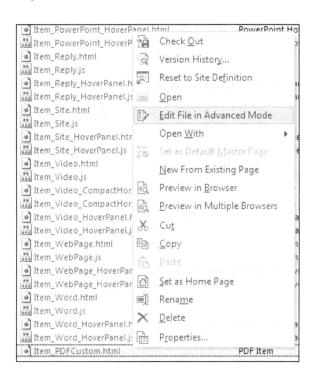

Rename the title:

```
<html xmlns:mso="urn:schemas-microsoft-com:office:offi
<head>
<title>PDF Customized Item</title>

<!--[if gte mso 9]><xml>
<mso:CustomDocumentProperties>
<mso:TemplateHidden msdt:dt="string">0</mso:TemplateHi
<mso:MasterPageDescription msdt:dt="string">Displays a
<mso:ContentTypeId msdt:dt="string">0x0101002039C03B61
<mso:TargetControlType msdt:dt="string">;#SearchResult
<mso:HtmlDesignAssociated msdt:dt="string">1</mso:Html
<mso:ManagedPropertyMapping msdt:dt="string">&#39;Titl
<mso:HtmlDesignConversionSucceeded msdt:dt="string">Tr
<mso:HtmlDesignStatusAndPreview msdt:dt="string">http:
</mso:CustomDocumentProperties>
</xml><![endif]-->
</head>
```

Change the hoverURL:

```
<body>
  <div id="Item PDF">
<!--#_
    if(!$isNull(ctx.CurrentItem) && !$isNull(ctx.ClientControl)){
        var id = ctx.ClientControl.get_nextUniqueId();
        var itemId = id + Srch.U.Ids.item;
        var hoverId = id + Srch.U.Ids.hover;
        var hoverUrl = "~sitecollection/_catalogs/masterpage/Display Templates/Search/Item_PDFCustom_HoverPanel.js";
        $setResultItem(itemId, ctx.CurrentItem);
        var k = ctx.DataProvider.get_currentQueryState().k;
        if(!Srch.U.e(k)){
            ctx.CurrentItem.csr_Path = ctx.CurrentItem.Path + "#search=" + $urlKeyValueEncode(k);
        }
        ctx.CurrentItem.csr_Icon = Srch.U.getIconUrlByFileExtension(ctx.CurrentItem);
        ctx.CurrentItem.csr_OpenApp = "word";
        ctx.currentItem_ShowHoverPanelCallback = Srch.U.getShowHoverPanelCallback(itemId, hoverId, hoverUrl);
        ctx.currentItem_HideHoverPanelCallback = Srch.U.getHideHoverPanelCallback();
```

Replace this line:

ctx.CurrentItem.csr_OpenControl = "PdfFile.OpenDocuments";

With this one:

ctx.CurrentItem.csr_OpenApp = "word";

```
if(!Srch.U.e(k)){
    ctx.CurrentItem.csr_Path = ctx.CurrentItem.Path + "#search=" + $urlKeyValueEncode(k);
}
ctx.CurrentItem.csr_Icon = Srch.U.getIconUrlByFileExtension(ctx.CurrentItem);
ctx.CurrentItem.csr_OpenControl = "PdfFile.OpenDocuments";
ctx.currentItem_ShowHoverPanelCallback = Srch.U.getShowHoverPanelCallback(itemId, hoverId, hoverUrl);
ctx.currentItem_HideHoverPanelCallback = Srch.U.getHideHoverPanelCallback();
```

```
if(!Srch.U.e(k)){
    ctx.CurrentItem.csr_Path = ctx.CurrentItem.Path + "#search=" + $urlKeyValueEncode(k);
}
ctx.CurrentItem.csr_Icon = Srch.U.getIconUrlByFileExtension(ctx.CurrentItem);
ctx.CurrentItem.csr_OpenApp = "word";
ctx.currentItem_ShowHoverPanelCallback = Srch.U.getShowHoverPanelCallback(itemId, hoverId, hoverUrl);
ctx.currentItem_HideHoverPanelCallback = Srch.U.getHideHoverPanelCallback();
```

Save the file.

This handles the opening of the PDF document in the browser.
Now for the preview.

Locate Item_Word_HoverPanel.html. Right-click and select copy:

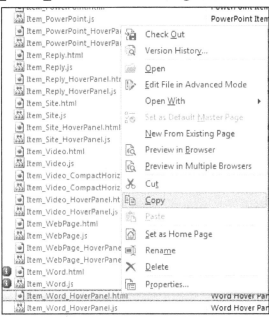

Right-click and select Paste:

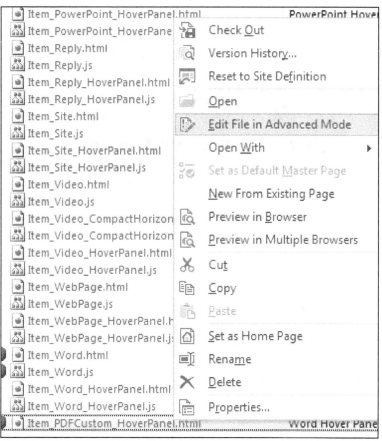

Rename the copied file (should be the same name you used for the hoverUrl value):

Right-click the new file and select Edit File in Advanced Mode:

Item_PowerPoint_HoverPanel.html		PowerPoint Hove
Item_PowerPoint_HoverPane	⏏	Check Out
Item_Reply.html	⊡	Version History...
Item_Reply.js		
Item_Reply_HoverPanel.html	⊡	Reset to Site Definition
Item_Reply_HoverPanel.js	⊡	Open
Item_Site.html		
Item_Site.js	⊳	Edit File in Advanced Mode
Item_Site_HoverPanel.html		Open With ▶
Item_Site_HoverPanel.js	⊡	Set as Default Master Page
Item_Video.html		
Item_Video.js		New From Existing Page
Item_Video_CompactHorizon	⊡	Preview in Browser
Item_Video_CompactHorizon	⊡	Preview in Multiple Browsers
Item_Video_HoverPanel.html		
Item_Video_HoverPanel.js	✂	Cut
Item_WebPage.html	⊡	Copy
Item_WebPage.js		
Item_WebPage_HoverPanel.h	⊡	Paste
Item_WebPage_HoverPanel.j	⌂	Set as Home Page
Item_Word.html	⊡	Rename
Item_Word.js		
Item_Word_HoverPanel.html	✕	Delete
Item_Word_HoverPanel.js	⊡	Properties...
Item_PDFCustom_HoverPanel.html		Word Hover Pane

Change the title:

```
<html xmlns:mso="urn:schemas-microsoft-com:office:office" xm
<head>
<title>PDF Custom Hover Panel</title>

<!--[if gte mso 9]><xml>
<mso:CustomDocumentProperties>
<mso:TemplateHidden msdt:dt="string">0</mso:TemplateHidden>
<mso:MasterPageDescription msdt:dt="string">Displays a resul
<mso:ContentTypeId msdt:dt="string">0x0101002039C03B61C64EC4
<mso:TargetControlType msdt:dt="string">;#SearchHoverPanel;#
<mso:HtmlDesignAssociated msdt:dt="string">1</mso:HtmlDesign
<mso:ManagedPropertyMapping msdt:dt="string">&#39;Title&#39;
<mso:HtmlDesignConversionSucceeded msdt:dt="string">True</ms
<mso:HtmlDesignStatusAndPreview msdt:dt="string">http://cova
</mso:CustomDocumentProperties>
</xml><![endif]-->
</head>
<body>
```

Save the Changes.

In your Search Center, select Site Settings from the Settings menu (gear). Under Site Collection Administration, click on Search Result Types:

Site Collection Administration
Recycle bin
Search Result Sources
Search Result Types
Search Query Rules
Search Schema
Search Settings
Search Configuration Import
Search Configuration Export
Site collection features

Scroll down and find the PDF entry. Select Copy from the drop-down menu:

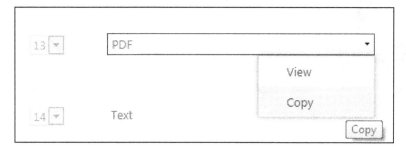

Give the type a unique name and select the PDF Customized Item as the display template:

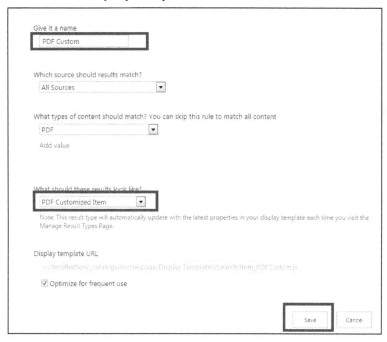

Click Save.

Now, the search results display previews using Office Web Apps:

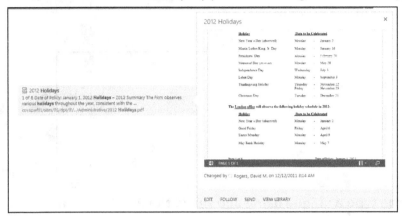

And the documents open in Adobe with the search term pass-through:

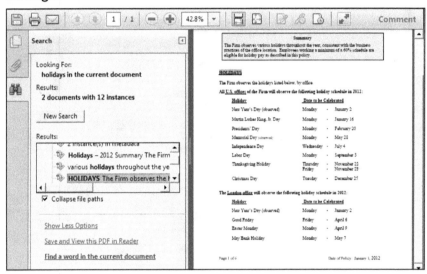

PDF Preview by Modifying Display Templates

This method of PDF previews involves the modification of search display templates. I found it better to modify the templates using SharePoint Designer 2013 although they are accessible through the SharePoint master page UI.

Fire up SharePoint Designer 2013 and Open the Search Center Site

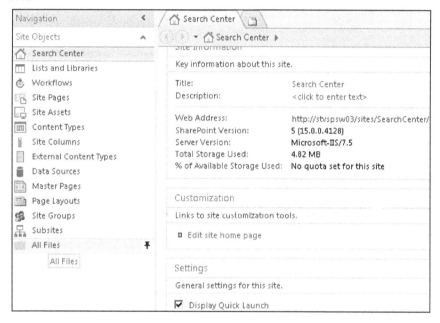

Click on All Files from the left-hand navigation

If you attempt to get the files from the Master Pages, you will not see any items once you get to the Display Templates folders.

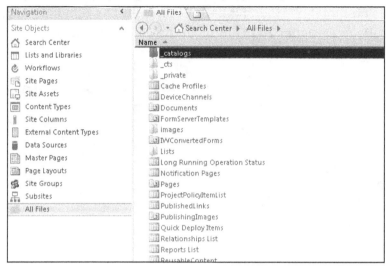

You see the list of all files in the main window.

Double-click on the _catalogs folder in the main window

This action displays the _catalogs structure under the left-hand navigation.

Expand the _catalogs folder, then the masterpage folder, and then the Display Templates folder.

Click on the Search folder under Display Templates

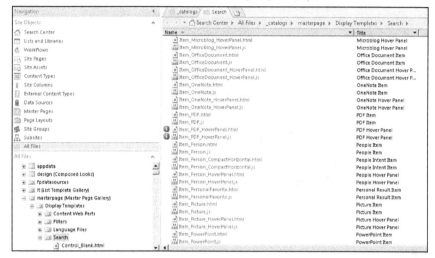

Right-click on Item_PDF_HoverPanel.html and select Edit File in Advanced Mode

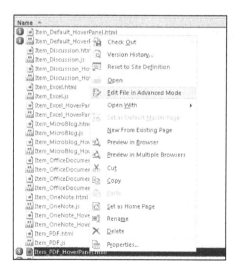

Paste the following code within the most inner <div>

```
<object data="  #= ctx.CurrentItem.Path =#  "
type="application/pdf" width="100%" height="500px" >
<p>It appears you don't have a PDF plugin for this browser/device.
You can <a href="  #= ctx.CurrentItem.Path =#  ">click here to
download the PDF file.</a></p>
</object>
```

```
<div id="Item PDF HoverPanel">
<!--#_
    var i = 0;
    var id = ctx.CurrentItem.csr_id;
    ctx.CurrentItem.csr_ShowFollowLink = true;
    ctx.CurrentItem.csr_ShowLastModifiedTime = true;
    ctx.CurrentItem.csr_ShowAuthors = true;
    ctx.CurrentItem.csr_ShowViewLibrary = true;
#-->
    <div class="ms-srch-hover-innerContainer ms-srch-hover-standardsize" id="_#= $htmlEncode(id + HP.ids.inner) =#_ ">
      <div class="ms-srch-hover-arrowBorder" id="_#= $htmlEncode(id + HP.ids.arrowBorder) =#_ "></div>
      <div class="ms-srch-hover-arrow" id="_#= $htmlEncode(id + HP.ids.arrow) =#_ "></div>
      <div class="ms-srch-hover-content" id="_#= $htmlEncode(id + HP.ids.content) =#_ " data-displaytemplate="PDFHoverPanel">
        <object data="_#= ctx.CurrentItem.Path =#_ " type="application/pdf" width="500px" height="680px" >
          <p>It appears you don't have a PDF plugin for this browser/device.
          You can <a href="_#= ctx.CurrentItem.Path =#_ ">click here to
          download the PDF file.</a></p>
        </object>
        <div id="_#= $htmlEncode(id + HP.ids.actions) =#_ " class="ms-srch-hover-actions">
          _#= ctx.RenderFooter(ctx) =#_
        </div>
      </div>
    </div>
</div>
</body>
</html>
```

I actually replaced the Render Header and Render Body divs with
the object code.

Save the file.
When saving the file, you may get a warning about breaking from
the site definition. Click OK. What happens behind the scenes is
that the HTML changes are incorporated into the javascript version of the template (Item_PDF_HoverPanel.js).

Test the results. Perform a search from your search center that produces PDF document results. Hover over the PDF document to see the preview:

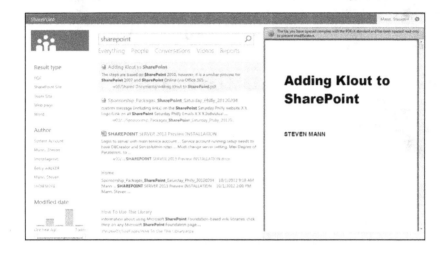

PDF Preview by Copying the Result Type (using Office Web Apps Server)

When using Office Web Apps Server with SharePoint 2013, there is an easier way to present PDF previews without having to modify the search display templates. This involves copying and modifying the PDF result type and have it render as a Word Item.

The first step is to navigate to your Search Center site settings:

Under Site Collection Administration, click on Search Result Types:

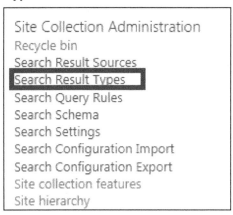

Scroll down and find the PDF entry under the Provided by the search service section. Select Copy from the drop-down menu:

On the Add Result Type page, rename the item and select Word Item under What should these results look like:

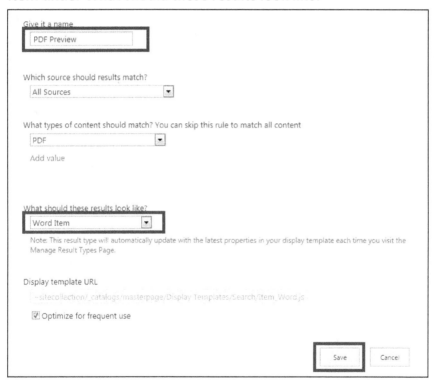

Click Save.

Run a full crawl and then perform a search that produces PDF entries. The hover preview now uses the Word App Viewer via Office Web Apps Server:

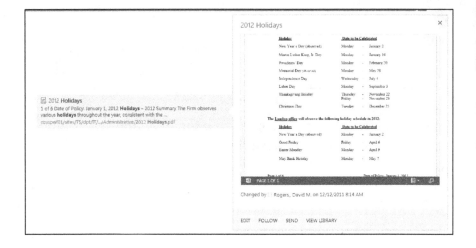

Conclusion

There are several different ways to handle the previewing of PDF search results in SharePoint 2013 by modifying the associated search display templates. The behaviors and user experience will vary depending on if you are using Office Web Apps Server 2013 or not. I hope this guide helped you understand the difference approaches and implementations that are possible.

Volume 8

How to Enhance the Search Box in SharePoint 2013

STEVEN MANN

How to Enhance the Search Box in SharePoint 2013

Copyright © 2013 by Steven Mann

Trademarks

Screenshots of Microsoft Products and Services

Warning and Disclaimer

Introduction

This guide steps through the various options and settings available for the Search Box web part which allow you to enhance the user search experience in SharePoint 2013. Search Suggestions are also covered.

Stay updated with my blog posts: www.SteveTheManMann.com

Reference links and source code is available on www.stevethemanmann.com:

Adding the Verticals Drop Down to the Search Box

Before the results pages are modified, the main page of the Search Center may be tweaked by modifying the Search Box web part on that page.

Navigate to your Search Center:

From the Settings menu, select Edit Page:

The page is presented in edit mode and is checked out to you automatically.

Click on Edit Web Part from the Search Box drop-down menu:

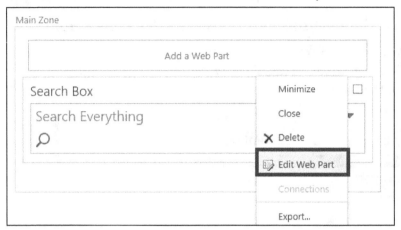

The Search Box Properties pane appears to the right of the page.

Select the Turn on drop-down Search Navigation option.

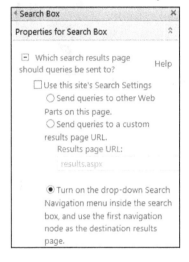

Click OK:

Check in the page:

Publish the page:

Now the user has an option to search within a defined context and navigate directly to that results page. These were previously named "scopes". Clicking Enter or clicking on the search button (magnifying glass) sends the query to the Everything page (re-sults.aspx).

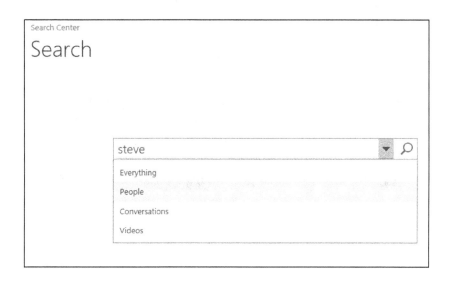

Displaying Links Next to the Search Box

You may modify the Search Box web part properties to display certain links next to the search box:

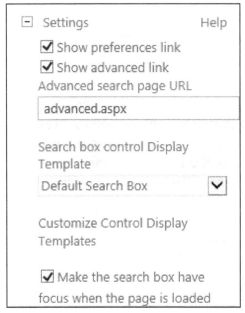

The Show preferences link option displays a link next to the Search Box where users may modify their search experience. The Show advanced link also displays a link to the right of the Search Box and navigates the user to the advanced search page.

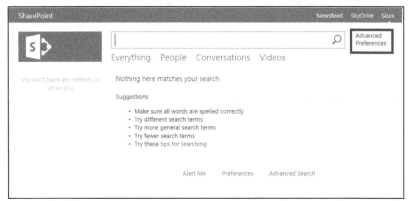

Setting Focus on the Search Box

In the Settings section of the Search Box web part properties, there is an option to set the focus behavior:

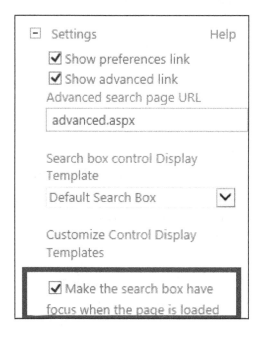

The **Make the search box have focus when the page is loaded** option places the cursor inside the search box so the user does not have to click inside to make a change.

Adding Suggestions to the Search Box

Suggestions Overview

bike|	$\mathcal{P}$
Bike Wash - Dissolver	
All-Purpose **Bike** Stand	
Hitch Rack - 4-**Bike**	
Mountain **Bike** Socks, L	
Mountain **Bike** Socks, M	

Suggestions are words or phrases that appear automatically when a user is typing search terms into a search box. Suggestions are enabled by default in both the Search Service Application and the Search Box web parts.

SharePoint automatically adds terms to the internal suggestion list based on user search actions. Once a term has been searched/queried and a result clicked a total of six (6) times, that term becomes part of the suggestion list.

This allows the suggestions to grow organically within your organization based on user past user search experiences. However, you may also add a list of suggestions to SharePoint to use. The sections to follow show you how to do just that.

When you add a list of suggestions to the Search Service Application, all previous suggestions are removed. Therefore, it is a good idea to start off with a suggestion list before going live with your new Search Center.

Create a Suggestion File

A suggestion file is just a text file that contains a word or phrase on each line. It may be anything that you feel will help your user search content. Some ideas include listing out products, clients/customers, contacts, etc. and using those values in the suggestion text file. For example purposes, I am going to list out all of the product names from the AdventureWorks sample database:

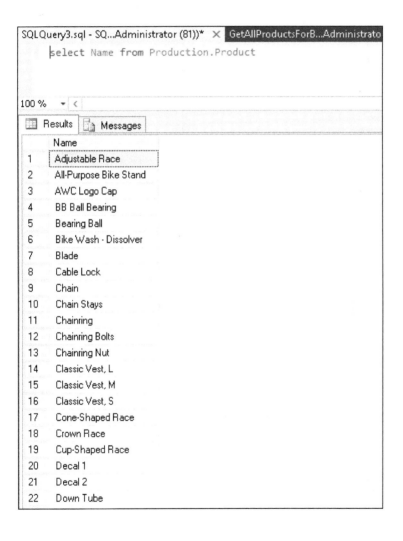

Copy and paste the list into a text file:

```
Suggestions.txt - Notepad
File  Edit  Format  View  Help
Adjustable Race
All-Purpose Bike Stand
AWC Logo Cap
BB Ball Bearing
Bearing Ball
Bike Wash - Dissolver
Blade
Cable Lock
Chain
Chain Stays
Chainring
Chainring Bolts
Chainring Nut
Classic Vest, L
Classic Vest, M
Classic Vest, S
Cone-Shaped Race
Crown Race
Cup-Shaped Race
Decal 1
Decal 2
Down Tube
External Lock Washer 1
External Lock Washer 2
External Lock Washer 3
External Lock Washer 4
External Lock Washer 5
External Lock Washer 6
External Lock Washer 7
External Lock Washer 8
External Lock Washer 9
Fender Set - Mountain
Flat Washer 1
Flat Washer 2
Flat Washer 3
Flat Washer 4
Flat Washer 5
Flat Washer 6
Flat Washer 7
```

Save the text file and get ready for import.

Import the Suggestion File

To import a suggestion file, navigate to your Search Service Application and click on Query Suggestions under the Queries and Results section of the left-hand navigation:

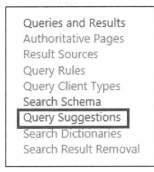

Click on the Import from text file link on the Query Suggestion Settings page:

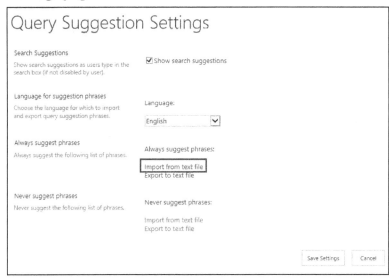

Click the Browse button to locate and select your suggestion text file:

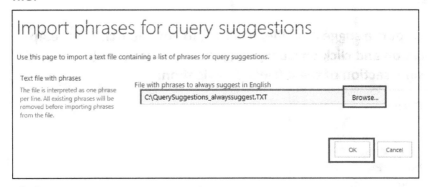

Click OK.

For good measure, click Save Settings:

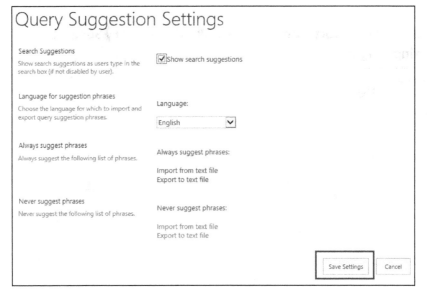

Process Query Suggestions

After the suggestions are imported, they will not appear until they are processed. They are processed via a timer job in SharePoint.

So instead of holding your breath to see the suggestions work, navigate to Central Administration and click on Monitoring from the left-hand navigation:

Click on Review job definitions under Timer Jobs:

On the Job Definitions page, scroll down to the bottom and click the arrow to go to the next page:

1-100 ▸

Scroll up on the next page and click on the Prepare Query Suggestions:

Title
My Site Instantiation Interactive Request Queue
My Site Instantiation Non-Interactive Request Queue
My Site Instantiation Non-Interactive Request Queue
My Site Second Instantiation Interactive Request Queue
My Site Second Instantiation Interactive Request Queue
Notification Timer Job c02c63c2-12d8-4ec0-b678-f05c7e00570e
Notification Timer Job c02c63c2-12d8-4ec0-b678-f05c7e00570e
Password Management
Performance Metric Provider
Persisted Navigation Term Set Synchronization
Persisted Navigation Term Set Synchronization
Prepare query suggestions
Product Version Job
Query Classification Dictionary Update for Search Application Search Service Application.
Query Logging
Rebalance crawl store partitions for Search Service Application

On the Edit Timer Job page, click Run Now:

The time job runs fairly quickly. You may view the results as explained in the next section.

View Suggestion Results

Navigate to your Search Center and type in a few letters that match some of your suggestion words/phrases:

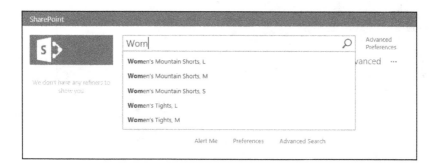

The matching suggestions appear under the Search Box. You may modify the suggestion behavior as explained in the next section.

Configuring Suggestions in the Search Box Web Part

By default the Search Box is set to show suggestions. You may also elect to show people name suggestions. This provides functionality similar to an auto-complete. You may configure how many suggestions appear and how long it takes to show suggestions based on the number of minimum characters configured.

```
[-]  Query Suggestions          Help

      ✔ Show suggestions
      ☐ Show people name
      suggestions

      Number of query suggestions
      ┌──────────────────────────┐
      │ 5                        │
      └──────────────────────────┘

      Minimum number of characters
      ┌──────────────────────────┐
      │ 2                        │
      └──────────────────────────┘

      Suggestions delay (in
      milliseconds)
      ┌──────────────────────────┐
      │ 100                      │
      └──────────────────────────┘

      ✔ Show personal favorite results
      Number of personal favorites
      ┌──────────────────────────┐
      │ 3                        │
      └──────────────────────────┘
```

The Search Box web part on each results page in your Search Center may be modified to change the behavior of suggestions and thus modify the user experience.

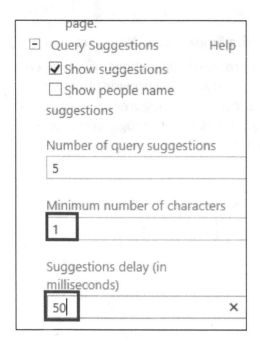

I like changing the minimum characters to 1 and the suggestions delay to 50 milliseconds. This allows the suggestions to appear quicker.

Volume 9

Synonyms and Sugar in SharePoint 2013 Search

STEVEN MANN

Synonyms and Sugar in SharePoint 2013 Search

Copyright © 2013 by Steven Mann

Trademarks

Screenshots of Microsoft Products and Services

Warning and Disclaimer

Introduction

This guide discusses the use of the search thesaurus, spelling words, and suggestions in SharePoint 2013 Search.

Stay updated with my blog posts: www.SteveTheManMann.com

Reference links and source code is available on www.stevethemanmann.com:

Adding a Thesaurus for Synonym Results

Synonyms Overview

When people search for items, they may use familiar terms or acronyms accordingly. However, the content may have terms spelled out or contain similar words as the search term but not the same word.

For example, if I search for "Philadelphia" but some content uses "Philly", I won't see those results. Similarly, if I search for "GE" but some content uses "General Electric", I won't see those results either.

This is where synonyms come into play. You may generate and upload a thesaurus file that contains pairs of terms such that when the first term is searched, the second term is also searched.

Create a Thesaurus File

A thesaurus file is a comma separated file which contains three columns: Key, Synonym, and Language. The Language column is optional and therefore your file technically could only contain pairs of synonyms.

An example of thesaurus file contents is as follows:

Key,Synonym,Language

IE,Internet Explorer

Internet Explorer,IE

HR, Human Resources

Human Resources, HR

Notice there is no "vice-versa" implied and therefore for each pair you may want to include the opposite order. Think of it as "when I search for this", "also include this".

To create a thesaurus file, simply open a text editor, add the header, and then go to town adding pairs of synonyms:

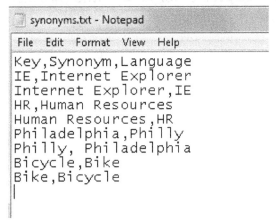

Save the file as a .csv file.

Import a Thesaurus File

In order to import your thesaurus file, you need to use PowerShell.

Launch the SharePoint 2013 Management Console and enter the following two command lines (using your own path for the -FileName parameter):

$ssa= Get-SPEnterpriseSearchServiceApplication

Import-SPEnterpriseSearchThesaurus -SearchApplication $ssa -Filename \\sp2013srv\c$\ThesaurusFile.csv

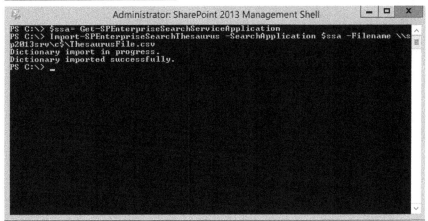

The thesaurus file is imported.

Test Synonyms in Search

To test the thesaurus file, simply search for various synonyms that the file contains. I knew with my example external data, that "Bike" was used often but "Bicycle" was not. I included these synonyms in my thesaurus file. Now when I search for Bicycle, I retrieve results that include Bike:

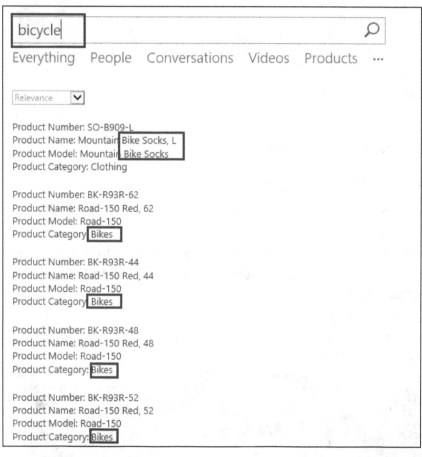

Adding Spelling Words

When looking to summarize the use of spelling words and show examples of the Did You Mean? functionality in SharePoint 2013 Search, I realized that Microsoft MVP, Waldek Mastykarz, already had this topic well summarized on his blog (http://blog.mastykarz.nl). Therefore, with his permission, I have adapted content from his blog post "SharePoint 2013 Query Spelling Inclusions for the masses" to complete this section.

SharePoint 2013 Search provides you with the query spelling suggestion capability that suggest correcting spelling mistakes in search queries. By default this capability is configured to automatically build the spelling suggestions dictionary. By changing the configuration settings it is possible to manually maintain the query spelling suggestions dictionary.

Spelling Words Overview

One of the biggest investments in SharePoint 2013 was the integration of the enterprise-class search engine, previously known as FAST, with the SharePoint Search engine. As a result SharePoint 2013 Search offers us top of the class search capabilities.

Among all the different search-related capabilities of SharePoint 2013 Search are query spelling suggestions – also known as 'did you mean'. Whenever you enter a search query, SharePoint 2013 Search will check if all words have been spelled correctly and if not, it will suggest the correct spelling.

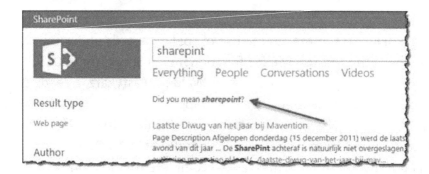

And while the query spelling suggestions do work by default, there are some challenges to how they are configured.

Query Spelling Suggestions

SharePoint 2013 Search knows two types of query spelling suggestion dictionaries: a dynamic and a static one. The dynamic dictionary is maintained by SharePoint itself based on the content in the search index, while the static one is maintained by yourself. Out of the box SharePoint uses the dynamic query spelling suggestions dictionary.

For a term to become a part of the dynamic query spelling dictionary, it has to occur in at least 50 documents. The interesting part is however the content alignment process which is used by the dynamic dictionary and which is enabled by default. This process is triggered when the term that occurs the most in the search index has been found in the preconfigured number of documents (1000 by default; can be changed using PowerShell) and then the dictionary is built.

If you are interested in exploring the default configuration of query spelling suggestions you can use the following PowerShell snippet:

```
$ssa = Get-SPEnterpriseSearchServiceApplication

Get-SPEnterpriseSearchQuerySpellingCorrection -SearchApplication $ssa
```

```
                     Administrator: SharePoint 2013 Management Shell        _  □  x
PS C:\> $ssa = Get-SPEnterpriseSearchServiceApplication
PS C:\> Get-SPEnterpriseSearchQuerySpellingCorrection -SearchApplication $ssa

ContentAlignmentEnabled            : True
MaxDictionarySize                  : 100000
MaxProcessingTime                  : 06:00:00
DiacriticsInSuggestionsEnabled     : True
TermFrequencyThreshold             : 1000
SecurityTrimmingEnabled            : False
SpellingDictionary                 : Dynamic
```

What if, however, you don't want to rely on the standard process
of building query spelling suggestions dictionary and want to build
and maintain one yourself? The next sub-section explains how to
add or remove your own words from SharePoint 2013 Search.

Adding Spelling Words to Your Search Service

Adding spelling words to your search service first involves switch-
ing the spelling dictionary mode to static, and then adding spelling
words into the spelling term sets. This sub-section explains both of
these processes.

SharePoint 2013 uses two Global Term Sets called **Query Spelling
Exclusions** and **Query Spelling Inclusions** to define the query
spelling suggestions. Both Term Sets are ignored in the dynamic
mode however, so before you can start entering your own suggestions, you have to switch to the static dictionary.

To switch to the static query spelling suggestions dictionary you
have to run the following PowerShell snippet:

$ssa = Get-SPEnterpriseSearchServiceApplication

Set-SPEnterpriseSearchQuerySpellingCorrection -SearchApplication $ssa -
SpellingDictionary

This will change the query spelling suggestions dictionary mode to
static and with this SharePoint 2013 Search will start using your
values stored in the two Term Sets.

Configuring query spelling suggestions is easy and comes down to
creating new Terms under the **Query Spelling Exclusions** Term Set

(for words which you never want to have suggested) and the **Query Spelling Inclusions** Term Set (for words which SharePoint should suggest). There are a few rules when it comes to configuring query spelling suggestions:

1. a query spelling suggestion is a single word, so **SharePoint** is a correct suggestion but **Sharing Points** is not

2. when creating query spelling suggestions only the first level of Terms is taken into account. SharePoint 2013 Search expects a list of words that it can then use to detect spelling mistakes. Query spelling suggestions Terms are in no way a dictionary such as **SharePint > SharePoint**, where the Term **SharePoint** would be a child Term of **SharePint** denoting in a way that every time SharePoint 2013 Search stumbles upon **SharePint** in a search query it should suggest **SharePoint** instead. This part is done by SharePoint automatically without our help.

Processing Spelling Words

After you have entered your query spelling suggestions Terms, they won't appear directly in the search results however. Instead you have to wait for the **Search Custom Dictionaries Update** Timer Job to run or execute it manually yourself.

After the job has executed and the query spelling suggestions from the static dictionary have been processed they will be used in SharePoint search results.

Adding Suggestions to the Search Box

Suggestions Overview

bike|	$\mathcal{Q}$
Bike Wash - Dissolver	
All-Purpose **Bike** Stand	
Hitch Rack - 4-**Bike**	
Mountain **Bike** Socks, L	
Mountain **Bike** Socks, M	

Suggestions are words or phrases that appear automatically when a user is typing search terms into a search box. Suggestions are enabled by default in both the Search Service Application and the Search Box web parts.

SharePoint automatically adds terms to the internal suggestion list based on user search actions. Once a term has been searched/queried and a result clicked a total of six (6) times, that term becomes part of the suggestion list.

This allows the suggestions to grow organically within your organization based on user past user search experiences. However, you may also add a list of suggestions to SharePoint to use. The sections to follow show you how to do just that.

When you add a list of suggestions to the Search Service Application, all previous suggestions are removed. Therefore, it is a good idea to start off with a suggestion list before going live with your new Search Center.

Create a Suggestion File

A suggestion file is just a text file that contains a word or phrase on each line. It may be anything that you feel will help your user search content. Some ideas include listing out products, clients/customers, contacts, etc. and using those values in the suggestion text file. For example purposes, I am going to list out all of the product names from the AdventureWorks sample database:

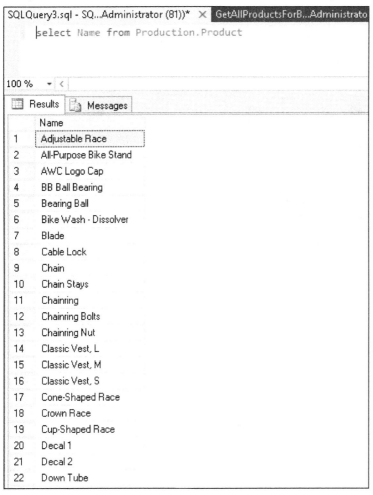

Copy and paste the list into a text file:

```
Suggestions.txt - Notepad
File   Edit   Format   View   Help
Adjustable Race
All-Purpose Bike Stand
AWC Logo Cap
BB Ball Bearing
Bearing Ball
Bike Wash - Dissolver
Blade
Cable Lock
Chain
Chain Stays
Chainring
Chainring Bolts
Chainring Nut
Classic Vest, L
Classic Vest, M
Classic Vest, S
Cone-Shaped Race
Crown Race
Cup-Shaped Race
Decal 1
Decal 2
Down Tube
External Lock Washer 1
External Lock Washer 2
External Lock Washer 3
External Lock Washer 4
External Lock Washer 5
External Lock Washer 6
External Lock Washer 7
External Lock Washer 8
External Lock Washer 9
Fender Set - Mountain
Flat Washer 1
Flat Washer 2
Flat Washer 3
Flat Washer 4
Flat Washer 5
Flat Washer 6
Flat Washer 7
```

Save the text file and get ready for import.

Import the Suggestion File

To import a suggestion file, navigate to your Search Service Application and click on Query Suggestions under the Queries and Results section of the left-hand navigation:

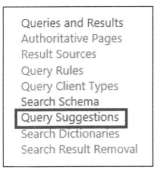

Click on the Import from text file link on the Query Suggestion Settings page:

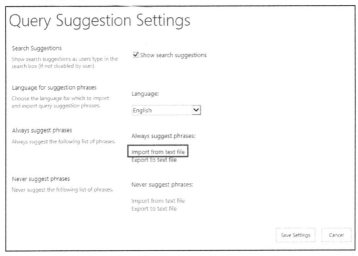

Click the Browse button to locate and select your suggestion text file:

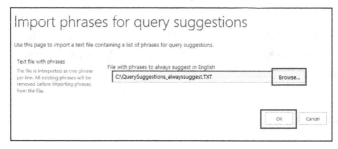

Import phrases for query suggestions

Use this page to import a text file containing a list of phrases for query suggestions.

Text file with phrases

The file is interpreted as one phrase per line. All existing phrases will be removed before importing phrases from the file.

File with phrases to always suggest in English

C:\QuerySuggestions_alwayssuggest.TXT   Browse...

OK   Cancel

Click OK.

For good measure, click Save Settings:

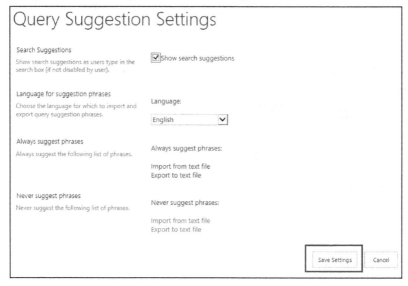

Query Suggestion Settings

Search Suggestions

Show search suggestions as users type in the search box (if not disabled by user).

☑ Show search suggestions

Language for suggestion phrases

Choose the language for which to import and export query suggestion phrases.

Language:

English ▾

Always suggest phrases

Always suggest the following list of phrases.

Always suggest phrases:

Import from text file
Export to text file

Never suggest phrases

Never suggest the following list of phrases.

Never suggest phrases:

Import from text file
Export to text file

Save Settings   Cancel

Process Query Suggestions

After the suggestions are imported, they will not appear until they are processed. They are processed via a timer job in SharePoint.

So instead of holding your breath to see the suggestions work, navigate to Central Administration and click on Monitoring from the left-hand navigation:

Click on Review job definitions under Timer Jobs:

On the Job Definitions page, scroll down to the bottom and click the arrow to go to the next page:

1-100 ▸

Scroll up on the next page and click on the Prepare Query Suggestions:

Title
My Site Instantiation Interactive Request Queue
My Site Instantiation Non-Interactive Request Queue
My Site Instantiation Non-Interactive Request Queue
My Site Second Instantiation Interactive Request Queue
My Site Second Instantiation Interactive Request Queue
Notification Timer Job c02c63c2-12d8-4ec0-b678-f05c7e00570e
Notification Timer Job c02c63c2-12d8-4ec0-b678-f05c7e00570e
Password Management
Performance Metric Provider
Persisted Navigation Term Set Synchronization
Persisted Navigation Term Set Synchronization
Prepare query suggestions
Product Version Job
Query Classification Dictionary Update for Search Application Search Service Application.
Query Logging
Rebalance crawl store partitions for Search Service Application

On the Edit Timer Job page, click Run Now:

Job Description	Prepares candidate queries for query suggestion and performs pre-computations for result block ranking.
Job Properties	Web application: N/A
This section lists the properties for this job.	Last run time: 4/19/2013 5:43 PM

Recurring Schedule

Use this section to modify the schedule specifying when the timer job will run. Daily, weekly, and monthly schedules also include a window of execution. The timer service will pick a random time within this interval to begin executing the job on each applicable server. This feature is appropriate for high-load jobs which run on multiple servers on the farm. Running this type of job on all the servers simultaneously might place an unreasonable load on the farm. To specify an exact starting time, set the beginning and ending times of the interval to the same value.

This timer job is scheduled to run:
- ○ Minutes   Starting every day between
- ○ Hourly   1 AM ⌄ 00 ⌄
- ● Daily   and no later than
- ○ Weekly   11 PM ⌄ 30 ⌄
- ○ Monthly

[Run Now] [Disable] [OK] [Cancel]

The time job runs fairly quickly. You may view the results as explained in the next section.

View Suggestion Results

Navigate to your Search Center and type in a few letters that match some of your suggestion words/phrases:

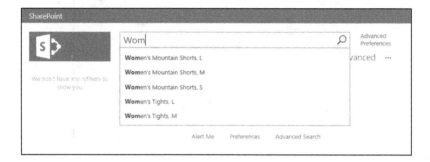

The matching suggestions appear under the Search Box. You may modify the suggestion behavior as explained in the next section.

Configuring Suggestions in the Search Box Web Part

By default the Search Box is set to show suggestions. You may also elect to show people name suggestions. This provides functionality similar to an auto-complete. You may configure how many suggestions appear and how long it takes to show suggestions based on the number of minimum characters configured.

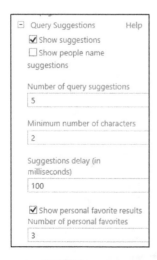

The Search Box web part on each results page in your Search Center may be modified to change the behavior of suggestions and thus modify the user experience.

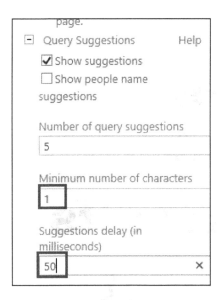

I like changing the minimum characters to 1 and the suggestions delay to 50 milliseconds. This allows the suggestions to appear quicker.

Volume 10

Enhancing Image and Picture Results in SharePoint 2013 Search

STEVEN MANN

Enhancing Image and Picture Results in SharePoint 2013

Copyright © 2013 by Steven Mann

Trademarks

Screenshots of Microsoft Products and Services

Warning and Disclaimer

Introduction

This guide walks through the configuration and behaviors of image/picture search results. Without any modifications to your search center and search service application, the crawling and presentation of image/picture items may not always be consistent.

Stay updated with my blog posts: www.SteveTheManMann.com

Reference links and source code is available on www.stevethemanmann.com:

Previewing of Images Not Stored in Picture Libraries

When images are stored in "regular" document libraries such as Site Assets, they are uploaded as documents. When the library is crawled, the results are the actual list item and not the image itself. Even if you add the Image or Picture content type to the library and modify the item, the result is still treated like a list item. The reason the images are coming back as items is because image file types such as .jpg and .gif are not in the list of the search file types. To correct this, follow the steps in this section.

Launch Central Admin:

Click on Manage service applications:

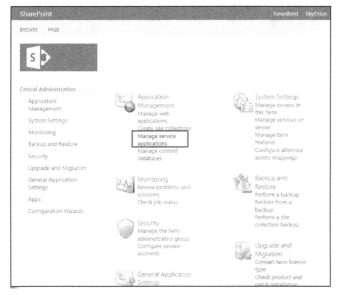

Click on Search Service Application:

On the left hand side click on File Types:

On the File Types page, click on New File Type:

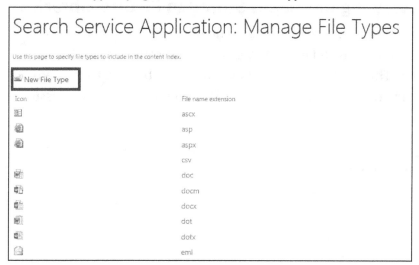

Enter an image file type such as jpg and click ok:

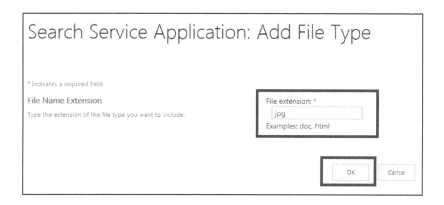

Repeat the process for other gif, png, tif, etc. or any other image types you want to handle.

Run a full crawl.

After the crawl is completed, the search results of the images should appear as their filename instead of a list item.

Previewing of Images Stored In Picture Libraries

After going through the steps in the previous section, it turns out even images stored in Picture Libraries are returned as files themselves. The hover works fine but you should be able to take advantage of the image result type. This section corrects that issue.

In your Search Center site collection select Site settings from the settings menu:

Under Site Collection Administration, click on Search Result Types:

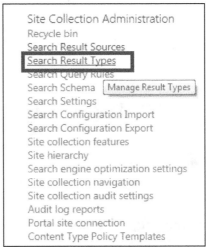

Scroll down and find Image. Use the drop-down menu and select Copy:

On the Add Result Type page, select Picture Item under What should these results look like?

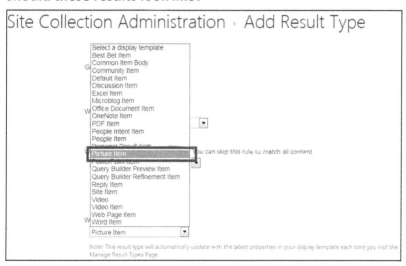

Click Save:

Run a search for an item in a Picture Library:

There is a preview image right in the results! That's great but that didn't happen in image results from other types of libraries - on to the next section.

Consistent UX for Images Results

After performing the steps in the previous sections, the results from a Picture Library and non-Picture Library look different. It is not consistent for the user:

You may correct this by editing the Picture Item display template (Item_Picture.html).

Fire up SharePoint Designer 2013 and Open the Search Center Site

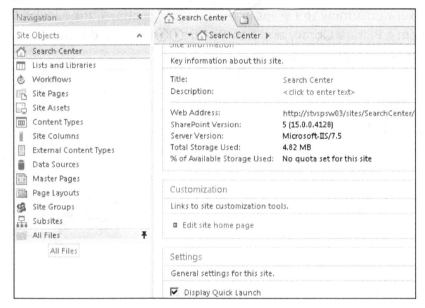

Click on All Files from the left-hand navigation

If you attempt to get the files from the Master Pages, you will not see any items once you get to the Display Templates folders.

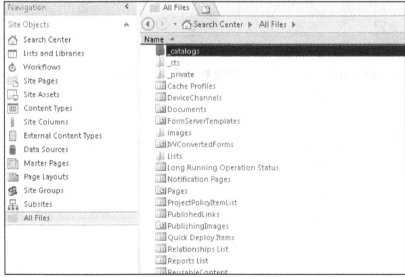

You see the list of all files in the main window.

Double-click on the _catalogs folder in the main window

This action displays the _catalogs structure under the left-hand navigation.

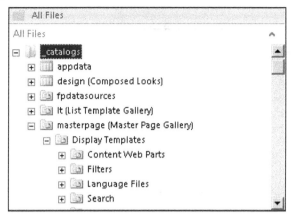

Expand the _catalogs folder, then the masterpage folder, and then the Display Templates folder.

Click on the Search folder under Display Templates

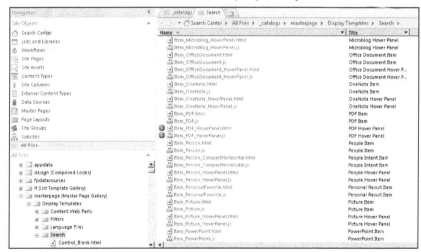

Locate the Item_Picture.html file, right click, and select Edit in Advanced Mode.

Simply add an else statement to the if in the middle of the code:

```
else {
ctx.CurrentItem.csr_PreviewImage = ctx.CurrentItem.Path;
}
```

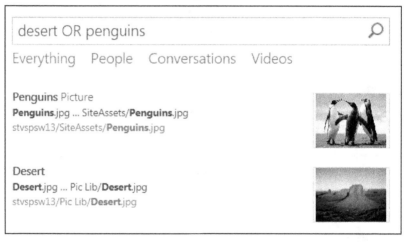

Save the file and run a search again:

desert OR penguins 🔍

Everything   People   Conversations   Videos

Penguins Picture
Penguins.jpg ... SiteAssets/**Penguins**.jpg
stvspsw13/SiteAssets/**Penguins**.jpg

Desert
Desert.jpg ... Pic Lib/**Desert**.jpg
stvspsw13/Pic Lib/**Desert**.jpg

Now all images that are returned have a preview image in the results!!!!

Displaying a Preview Image in the Image Search Result Hover Panel

Hovering over the image search results does not show a larger preview image:

Modify the Item_Picture_HoverPanel.html file and add the following code right before the first if statement:

```
<div class="ms-srch-hover-imageContainer">
<img id=" #= ctx.CurrentItem.csr_id =# " src=" #= $urlHtmlEn-
code(ctx.CurrentItem.Path) =# " onload="this.style.display='block';" />
</div>
```

Save the file and refresh the search results. A larger image shows in the hover now:

Displaying Image Results Horizontally (with Hover)

SharePoint 2013 contains templates to display both videos and people in a horizontal fashion presenting a nice presentation in the Everything search results. For an example of the Video horizontal display see the previous chapter.

It would be nice to also have this horizontal functionality for images as well as display the hover panel on the items (since the people and video horizontal displays do not incorporate the hover panel out-of-the-box).

Launch SharePoint Designer 2013 and navigate to the search center display templates (similar to the steps outlined in Appendix A).

Locate the Item_Picture.html, right-click and select Copy:

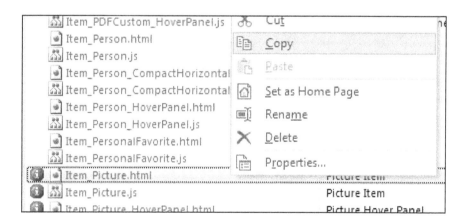

Right-click again and select Paste:

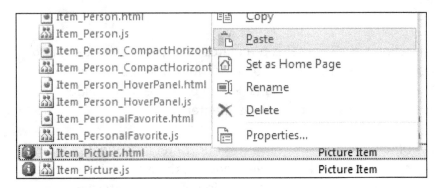

Rename the copied file to Item_Picture_CompactHorizontal:

	Item_PersonalFavorite.js
🛈 📄	Item_Picture.html
🛈 📊	Item_Picture.js
🛈 📄	Item_Picture_CompactHorizontal.html
📊	Item_Picture_copy(1).js
🛈 📄	Item_Picture_HoverPanel.html
🛈 📊	Item_Picture_HoverPanel.js

Right-click again and select Edit File in Advanced Mode:

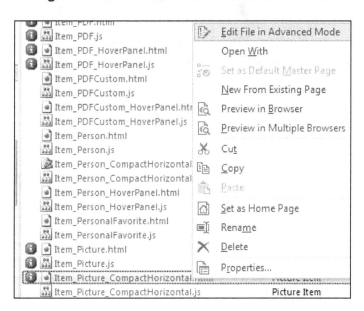

Rename the title and the main div id:

```
<html xmlns:mso="urn:schemas-microsoft-com:office:office" xmlns:msdt="
<head>
<title>Picture Horizontal</title>

<!--[if gte mso 9]><xml>
<mso:CustomDocumentProperties>
<mso:TemplateHidden msdt:dt="string">0</mso:TemplateHidden>
<mso:MasterPageDescription msdt:dt="string">Displays a result tailored
<mso:ContentTypeId msdt:dt="string">0x0101002039C03B61C64EC4A04F5361F3
<mso:TargetControlType msdt:dt="string">;#SearchResults;#</mso:TargetC
<mso:HtmlDesignAssociated msdt:dt="string">1</mso:HtmlDesignAssociated>
<mso:ManagedPropertyMapping msdt:dt="string">&#39;Title&#39;;:&#39;Titl
<mso:HtmlDesignStatusAndPreview msdt:dt="string">http://covspwf01/sites
<mso:HtmlDesignConversionSucceeded msdt:dt="string">True</mso:HtmlDesi
</mso:CustomDocumentProperties>
</xml><![endif]-->
</head>
<body>
    <div id="Item_Picture_CompactHorizontal">
<!--#
        if(!$isNull(ctx.CurrentItem) && !$isNull(ctx.ClientControl)){
            var id = ctx.ClientControl.get_nextUniqueId();
            var itemId = id + Srch.U.Ids.item;
            var hoverId = id + Srch.U.Ids.hover;
```

Add the following code as shown in the image below:

```
<!--#
if (!Srch.U.n(ctx.CurrentItem.ParentTableReference) &&
ctx.CurrentItem.ParentTableReference.TotalRows > 1) {
 #-->
```

```
<!--#
} else {
 #-->
```

```
      if(!$isNull(ctx.CurrentItem) && !$isNull(ctx.ClientControl)){
          var id = ctx.ClientControl.get_nextUniqueId();
          var itemId = id + Srch.U.Ids.item;
          var hoverId = id + Srch.U.Ids.hover;
          var hoverUrl = "~sitecollection/_catalogs/masterpage/Display Templates/Search/Item_Picture_HoverPanel.js";
          $setResultItem(itemId, ctx.CurrentItem);
          ctx.currentItem_ShowHoverPanelCallback = Srch.U.getShowHoverPanelCallback(itemId, hoverId, hoverUrl);
          ctx.currentItem_HideHoverPanelCallback = Srch.U.getHideHoverPanelCallback();
#-->
```

```
--#
          if (!Srch.U.n(ctx.CurrentItem.ParentTableReference) && ctx.CurrentItem.ParentTableReference.TotalRows > 1) {
-->
```

```
--#
          } else {
-->
```

```
--#
          <div id="_#= $htmlEncode(itemId) =#_" name="Item" data-displaytemplate="PictureItem" class="ms-srch-item" onmouseo
          if(!Srch.U.n(ctx.CurrentItem.PictureThumbnailURL) && !ctx.CurrentItem.IsContainer) {
              ctx.CurrentItem.csr_PathLength = Srch.U.pathTruncationLengthWithPreview;
              ctx.CurrentItem.csr_PreviewImage = ctx.CurrentItem.PictureThumbnailURL;
```

Scroll to the bottom and add an additional closing bracket:

```
_#-->
                    _#=ctx.RenderBody(ctx)=#_
                    <div id="_#= $htmlEncode(hoverId) =#_"
            </div>
<!--#_
            [  }  ]

            }
_#-->
        </div>
</body>
</html>
```

Between the if and the else that you pasted first, enter the following code as shown in the image below:

```
<div id="_#= $htmlEncode(itemId) =#_" name="Item" class="ms-srch-people-
intentItem" onmouseover="_#= ctx.currentItem_ShowHoverPanelCallback =#_"
onmouseout="_#= ctx.currentItem_HideHoverPanelCallback =#_">
<div id="ImageInfo">
<!--#_
var pathEncoded = $urlHtmlEncode(ctx.CurrentItem.Path);
var encodedName = $htmlEncode(ctx.CurrentItem.Title);
 _#-->

<ul id="ImageCard">
<li id="ImagePic">
<a clicktype="Result" href="_#= pathEncoded =#_" title="_#= encodedName =#_">
<img id="PicPreview" src="_#= pathEncoded =#_" height="80px" width="80px"/>
</a>
</li>
<li id="ImageTitle">
<div id="imageTitle" class="ms-textSmall ms-srch-ellipsis" title="_#= encodedName
=#_">_#= encodedName =#_</div>
</li>
</ul>
<div id="_#= $htmlEncode(hoverId) =#_" class="ms-srch-hover-
outerContainer"></div>
</div>
</div>
```

```
<!--#_
  #-->
                if (!Srch.U.n(ctx.CurrentItem.ParentTableReference) && ctx.CurrentItem.ParentTableReference.TotalRows
            <div id="_#= $htmlEncode(itemId) =#_" name="Item" class="ms-srch-people-intentItem" onmouseover="_#= ctx.
                <div id="ImageInfo">
<!--#_
                        var pathEncoded = $urlHtmlEncode(ctx.CurrentItem.Path);
                        var encodedName = $htmlEncode(ctx.CurrentItem.Title);
  #-->
               <ul id="ImageCard">
                  <li id="ImagePic">
                     <a clicktype="Result" href="_#= pathEncoded =#_" title="_#= encodedName =#_">
                        <img id="PicPreview" src="_#= pathEncoded =#_" height="80px" width="80px"/>
                     </a>
                  </li>
                  <li id="ImageTitle">
                     <div id="imageTitle" class="ms-textSmall ms-srch-ellipsis" title="_#= encodedName =#_">
                  </li>
               </ul>
               <div id="_#= $htmlEncode(hoverId) =#_" class="ms-srch-hover-outerContainer"></div>
            </div>
         </div>
<!--#_
  #-->
            } else {
```

Save the changes and then navigate to your Search Center.

From your Search Center site settings, select Search Query Rules from the Site Collection Administration section:

Site Collection Administration
Recycle bin
Search Result Sources
Search Result Types
Search Query Rules
Search Schema
Search Settings
Search Configuration Import
Search Configuration Export
Site collection features

Select the Local SharePoint Results (System):

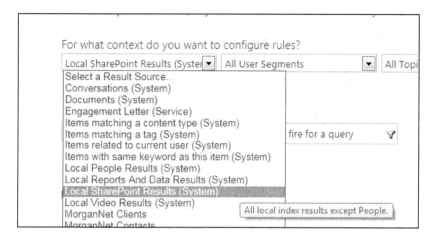

After the Query Rules load on the page, scroll down and find the Image entry. From the drop-down menu select Copy:

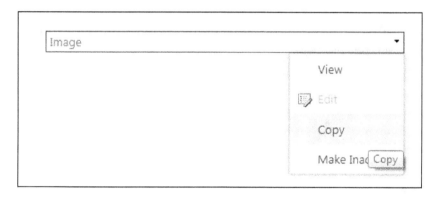

Change the Rule name:

Rule name

Image - Copy

Fires only on source Local SharePoint Results.

Advanced Query Text Match ▼

◯ Query matches this regular expression

◉ Query contains one of these phrases (semi-colon separated)

.gif;.jpg;.png;gif;image;images;jpg;photo;ph

◯ Query contains an entry in this dictionary

People Names ▼

The People Name dictionary uses People Search to support fuzzy matching.
Import from term store

Scroll down to the Actions sections and click on edit to edit the result block:

Actions

When your rule fires, it can enhance search results in three ways. It can add promoted results above the ranked results. It can also add blocks of additional results. Like normal results, these blocks can be promoted to always appear above ranked results or ranked so they only appear if highly relevant. Finally, the rule can change ranked results, such as tuning their ordering.

Promoted Results

Add Promoted Result

Result Blocks

Promoted (shown above ranked results in this order)
Images for "{subjectTerms}" edit remove

Add Result Block

Change ranked results by changing the query

Change the Query. (I was not getting expected results from the InternalFileType property. Therefore I changed my query filter to "(ContentType:PictureItem OR ContentType:Image)").

I also changed the amount of items to 6:

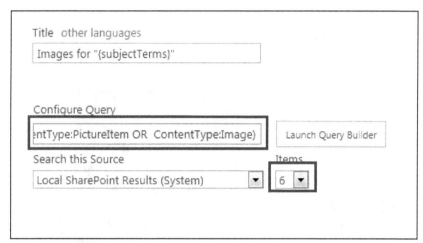

In the Settings select This block is always shown above core results and also change the Item Display Template to the new Picture Horizontal template:

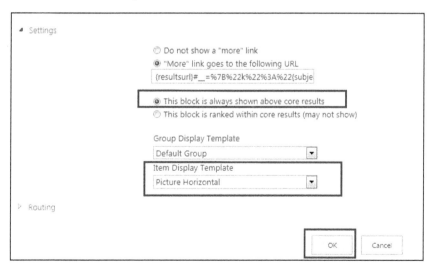

Click OK. Click Save on the Edit Query Rule page.

Navigate to your search page and peform a search for images:

Images for "computer"

04-05-07_1016.jpg 04-05-07_1017.jpg 04-05-07_1018.jpg 04-05-07_1423.jpg 04-05-07_1424.jpg 04-05-07_1425.jpg

SHOW MORE
About 408 results

The images display horizontally and the hover works as well:

computer image	04-05-07_1017.jpg	×

Picture Library List Item

Everything   People

Relevance ▼

Images for "computer"

04-05-07_1016.jpg   04-05-07_1017.jpg

SHOW MORE
About 408 results

Picture dimensions
480 x 640

Changed by ☐

OPEN   SEND   VIEW LIBRARY